Editor
Cristina Krysinski, M. Ed.

Editor in Chief
Karen J. Goldfluss, M.S. Ed.

Creative Director
Sarah M. Fournier

Cover Artist
Barbara Lorseyedi

Art Coordinator
Renée Mc Elwee

Imaging
Amanda R. Harter

Publisher
Mary D. Smith, M.S. Ed.

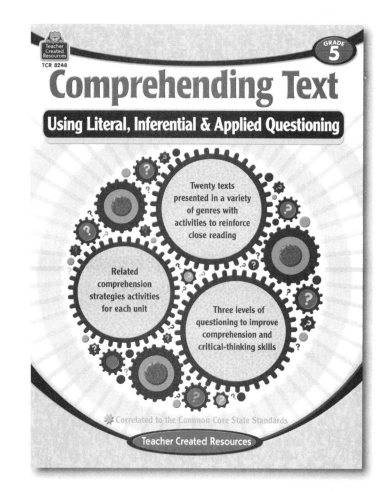

GRADE 5

TCR 8248

Comprehending Text
Using Literal, Inferential & Applied Questioning

Twenty texts presented in a variety of genres with activities to reinforce close reading

Related comprehension strategies activities for each unit

Three levels of questioning to improve comprehension and critical-thinking skills

Correlated to the Common Core State Standards

Teacher Created Resources

D1616834

CORRELATED TO COMMON CORE STANDARDS

For correlations to the Common Core State Standards, see page 109 of this book or visit *http://www.teachercreated.com/standards*.

Teacher Created Resources
6421 Industry Way
Westminster, CA 92683
www.teachercreated.com

ISBN: 978-1-4206-8248-9

© *2015 Teacher Created Resources*
Made in U.S.A.

Teacher Created Resources

Table of Contents

Introduction

Twenty different texts from a variety of genres are included in this reading comprehension resource. These may include humor, fantasy, myth/legend, folktale, mystery, adventure, suspense, fairy tale, play, fable, science fiction, poetry, and informational/nonfiction texts, such as a timetable, letter, report, procedure, poster, map, program, book cover, and cartoon.

Three levels of questions are used to indicate the reader's comprehension of each text.

One or more particular comprehension strategies have been chosen for practice with each text.

Each unit is five pages long and consists of the following resources and strategies:

- teacher information: includes the answer key and extension suggestions
- text page: text is presented on one full page
- activity page 1: covers literal and inferential questions
- activity page 2: covers applied questions
- applying strategies: focuses on a chosen comprehension strategy/strategies

Teacher Information

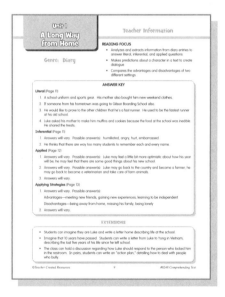

- **Reading Focus** states the comprehension skill emphasis for the unit.
- **Genre** is clearly indicated.
- **Answer Key** is provided. For certain questions, answers will vary, but suggested answers are given.
- **Extension Activities** suggest other authors or books titles. Other literacy activities relating to the text are suggested.

Text Page

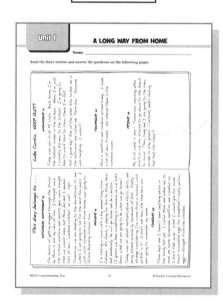

- The title of the text is provided.
- Statement is included in regard to the genre.
- Text is presented on a full page.

Activity Page 1

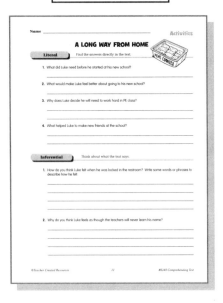

Activity Page 2

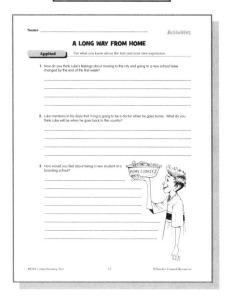

- **Literal** questions provide opportunities to practice locating answers in the text.

- **Inferential** questions provide opportunities to practice finding evidence in the text.

- **Applied** questions provide opportunities to practice applying prior knowledge.

Applying Strategies

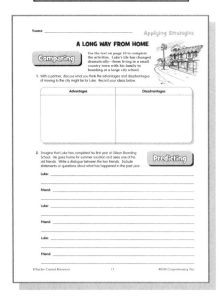

- Comprehension strategy focus is clearly labeled.

- Activities provide opportunities to utilize the particular strategy.

Types of Questions

Students are given **three types of questions** (all grouped accordingly) to assess their comprehension of a particular text in each genre:

- **Literal questions** are questions for which answers can be found directly in the text.

- **Inferential questions** are questions for which answers are implied in the text and require the reader to think a bit more deeply about what he or she has just read.

- **Applied questions** are questions that require the reader to think even further about the text and incorporate personal experiences and knowledge to answer them.

Answers for literal questions are always given and may be found on the Teacher Information pages. Answers for inferential questions are given when appropriate. Applied questions are best checked by the teacher following, or in conjunction with, a class discussion.

Comprehension Strategies

Several specific comprehension strategies have been selected for practice in this book.

Although specific examples have been selected, often other strategies, such as scanning, are used in conjunction with those indicated, even though they may not be stated. Rarely does a reader use only a single strategy to comprehend a text.

Strategy Definitions

Predicting	Prediction involves the students using illustrations, text, or background knowledge to help them construct meaning. Students might predict what texts could be about, what could happen, or how characters could act or react. Prediction may occur before, during, and after reading, and it can be adjusted during reading.
Making Connections	Students comprehend texts by linking their prior knowledge with the new information from the text. Students may make connections between the text and themselves, between the new text and other texts previously read, and between the text and real-world experiences.
Comparing	This strategy is closely linked to the strategy of making connections. Students make comparisons by thinking more specifically about the similarities and differences between the connections being made.
Sensory Imaging	Sensory imaging involves students utilizing all five senses to create mental images of passages in the text. Students also use their personal experiences to create these images. The images may help students make predictions, form conclusions, interpret information, and remember details.

Strategy Definitions (cont.)

Determining Importance/ Identifying Main Idea(s)

The strategy of determining importance is particularly helpful when students try to comprehend informational texts. It involves students determining the important theme or main idea of particular paragraphs or passages.

As students become effective readers, they will constantly ask themselves what is most important in a phrase, sentence, paragraph, chapter, or whole text. To determine importance, students will need to use a variety of information, such as the purpose for reading, their knowledge of the topic, background experiences and beliefs, and understanding of the text format.

Skimming

Skimming is the strategy of looking quickly through texts to gain a general impression or overview of the content. Readers often use this strategy to quickly assess whether a text, or part of it, will meet their purpose. Because this book deals predominantly with comprehension after reading, skimming has not been included as one of the major strategies.

Scanning

Scanning is the strategy of quickly locating specific details, such as dates, places, or names, or those parts of the text that support a particular point of view. Scanning is often used, but not specifically mentioned, when used in conjunction with other strategies.

Synthesizing/Sequencing

Synthesizing is the strategy that enables students to collate a range of information in relation to the text. Students recall information, order details, and piece information together to make sense of the text. Synthesizing/sequencing helps students to monitor their understanding. Synthesizing involves connecting, comparing, determining importance, posing questions, and creating images.

Summarizing/Paraphrasing

Summarizing involves the processes of recording key ideas, main points, or the most important information from a text. Summarizing or paraphrasing reduces a larger piece of text to the most important details.

Genre Definitions

Fiction and Poetry

Science Fiction These stories include backgrounds or plots based upon possible technology or inventions, experimental medicine, life in the future, environments drastically changed, alien races, space travel, genetic engineering, dimensional portals, or changed scientific principles. Science fiction encourages readers to suspend some of their disbelief and examine alternate possibilities.

Suspense Stories of suspense aim to make the reader feel fear, disgust, or uncertainty. Many suspense stories have become classics. These include *Frankenstein* by Mary Shelley, *Dracula* by Bram Stoker, and *Dr. Jekyll and Mr. Hyde* by Robert Louis Stevenson.

Mystery Stories from this genre focus on the solving of a mystery. Plots of mysteries often revolve around a crime. The hero must solve the mystery, overcoming unknown forces or enemies. Stories about detectives, police, private investigators, amateur sleuths, spies, thrillers, and courtroom dramas usually fall into this genre.

Fable A fable is a short story that states a moral. Fables often use talking animals or animated objects as the main characters. The interaction of the animals or animated objects reveals general truths about human nature.

Fairy Tale These tales are usually about elves, dragons, goblins, fairies, or magical beings and are often set in the distant past. Fairy tales usually begin with the phrase "Once upon a time . . ." and end with the words ". . . and they lived happily ever after." Charms, disguises, and talking animals may also appear in fairy tales.

Fantasy A fantasy may be any text or story removed from reality. Stories may be set in nonexistent worlds, such as an elf kingdom, on another planet, or in alternate versions of the known world. The characters may not be human (dragons, trolls, etc.) or may be humans who interact with non-human characters.

Folktale Stories that have been passed from one generation to the next by word of mouth rather than by written form are folktales. Folktales may include sayings, superstitions, social rituals, legends, or lore about the weather, animals, or plants.

Play Plays are specific pieces of drama, usually enacted on a stage by actors dressed in makeup and appropriate costumes.

Adventure Exciting events and actions feature in these stories. Character development, themes, or symbolism are not as important as the actions or events in an adventure story.

Humor Humor involves characters or events that promote laughter, pleasure, or humor in the reader.

Genre Definitions *(cont.)*

Fiction and Poetry *(cont.)*

Poetry
This genre utilizes rhythmic patterns of language. The patterns include meter (high- and low-stressed syllables), syllabication (the number of syllables in each line), rhyme, alliteration, or a combination of these. Poems often use figurative language.

Myth
A myth explains a belief, practice, or natural phenomenon and usually involves gods, demons, or supernatural beings. A myth does not necessarily have a basis in fact or a natural explanation.

Legend
Legends are told as though the events were actual historical events. Legends may or may not be based on an elaborated version of a historical event. Legends are usually about human beings, although gods may intervene in some way throughout the story.

Nonfiction

Report
Reports are written documents describing the findings of an individual or group. They may take the form of a newspaper report, sports report, or police report, or a report about an animal, person, or object.

Letter
These are written conversations sent from one person to another. Letters usually begin with a greeting, contain the information to be related, and conclude with a farewell signed by the sender.

Procedure
Procedures tell how to make or do something. They use clear, concise language and command verbs. A list of materials required to complete the procedure is included, and the instructions are set out in easy-to-follow steps.

Biography
A biography is an account of a person's life written by another person. The biography may be about the life of a celebrity or a historical figure.

Diary
A diary entry contains a description of daily events in a person's life.

Persuasive/Exposition
This nonfiction genre is written to persuade others to a particular point of view. Expositions begin with a statement of the writer's position on an issue. This is followed by arguments with supporting details, such as evidence and examples. Rhetorical questions are included in expositions to encourage the reader to agree with the writer's point of view.

Journalistic Writing
Usually formal and structured, journalistic writing aims to present information accurately, clearly, and efficiently rather than to present and develop an individual writer's style. Journalistic writing is usually written in the third person.

Other **informational texts**, such as **timetables**, are excellent sources to teach and assess comprehension skills. Others may include **diagrams**, **graphs**, **advertisements**, **maps**, **plans**, **tables**, **charts**, **lists**, **posters**, and **programs**.

READING FOCUS

- Analyzes and extracts information from diary entries to answer literal, inferential, and applied questions

- Makes predictions about a character in a text to create dialogue

- Compares the advantages and disadvantages of two different settings

ANSWER KEY

Literal (Page 11)

1. A school uniform and sports gear. His mother also bought him new weekend clothes.

2. If someone from his hometown was going to Gilson Boarding School also.

3. He would like to prove to the other children that he's a fast runner. He used to be the fastest runner at his old school.

4. Luke asked his mother to make him muffins and cookies because the food at the school was inedible. He shared the treats.

Inferential (Page 11)

1. Answers will vary. Possible answer(s): humiliated, angry, hurt, embarrassed.

2. He thinks that there are way too many students to remember each and every name.

Applied (Page 12)

1. Answers will vary. Possible answer(s): Luke may feel a little bit more optimistic about how his year will be; he may feel that there are some good things about his new school.

2. Answers will vary. Possible answer(s): Luke may go back to the country and become a farmer; he may go back to become a veterinarian and take care of farm animals.

3. Answers will vary.

Applying Strategies (Page 13)

1. Answers will vary. Possible answer(s):

   Advantages—meeting new friends, gaining new experiences, learning to be independent

   Disadvantages—being away from home, missing his family, being lonely

2. Answers will vary.

EXTENSIONS

- Students can imagine they are Luke and write a letter home describing life at the school.

- Imagine that 10 years have passed. Students can write a letter from Luke to Yong in Vietnam, describing the last five years of his life since he left school.

- The class can hold a discussion regarding how Luke should respond to the person who locked him in the restroom. In pairs, students can write an "action plan," detailing how to deal with people who bully.

A LONG WAY FROM HOME

Name _____

Read the diary entries and answer the questions on the following pages.

This diary belongs to . . .

SATURDAY, SEPTEMBER 17

Five hours of getting dragged through the stores by Mom is not my idea of fun. I thought once the school uniform and sports gear were bought that we would leave, but Mom decided I needed lots of new "weekend clothes" as well. Ugh!

Tomorrow we are heading to the dormitories to see where I am going to live for the next five years. I just wish someone else from home was going to Gilson Boarding School, too.

MONDAY 19

I'm sharing a room with a boy named Yong from Vietnam. His family is paying for him to study here, but eventually, he will go home and be a doctor. (I guess we have something in common, as we both know what we are going to be when we go home.)

Today was all about multiplication facts, bells, and being shoved around by hundreds of kids. Pretty strange considering I've come from a school with 63 kids in it! I don't see how the teachers are ever going to remember my name.

TUESDAY 20

Three days and I haven't seen anything edible in the dining hall yet. I called Mom and asked her to send me some homemade muffins and cookies so I don't fade away. What I would give for some fresh scrambled eggs for breakfast—really yellow eggs—straight from the chicken.

Luke Curtin. KEEP OUT!

WEDNESDAY 21

Today was our first PE class. Back home, I'm the fastest runner in the school. Here, I'm just a country kid new to the school. I'm going to have to work hard to show them I'm fast.

Not a good day! One of the older kids locked me in the restroom and called me "farm boy." Everyone was laughing. I wasn't!

THURSDAY 22

Mom's muffins and cookies arrived today. I made a lot of new friends. We shared them in the common room.

FRIDAY 23

My first week is over! Tomorrow morning, after practice, we are allowed to go down to the beach to swim. Then, Yong and I are going to the video arcade to play games. (Certainly beats helping Dad feed the sheep!)

A LONG WAY FROM HOME

| Literal | Find the answers directly in the text. |

1. What did Luke need before he started at his new school?

_____

2. What would make Luke feel better about going to his new school?

_____

3. Why does Luke decide he will need to work hard in PE class?

_____

_____

4. What helped Luke to make new friends at the school?

_____

_____

| Inferential | Think about what the text says. |

1. How do you think Luke felt when he was locked in the restroom? Write some words or phrases to describe how he felt.

_____

_____

_____

2. Why do you think Luke feels as though the teachers will never learn his name?

_____

_____

_____

A LONG WAY FROM HOME

Applied   Use what you know about the text and your own experience.

1. How do you think Luke's feelings about moving to the city and going to a new school have changed by the end of the first week?

_____

_____

_____

_____

2. Luke mentions in his diary that Yong is going to be a doctor when he goes home. What do you think Luke will be when he goes back to the country?

_____

_____

_____

_____

3. How would you feel about being a new student at a boarding school?

_____

_____

_____

_____

_____

_____

MOM'S COOKIES

A LONG WAY FROM HOME

Use the text on page 10 to complete the activities. Luke's life has changed dramatically—from living in a small country town with his family to boarding at a large city school.

1. With a partner, discuss what you think the advantages and disadvantages of moving to the city might be for Luke. Record your ideas below.

Advantages	Disadvantages

2. Imagine that Luke has completed his first year at Gilson Boarding School. He goes home for summer vacation and sees one of his old friends. Write a dialogue between the two friends. Include statements or questions about what has happened in the past year.

Luke: _____

_____

Friend: _____

_____

Luke: _____

_____

Friend: _____

_____

Luke: _____

_____

Friend: _____

_____

Genre: Humor

READING FOCUS

- Analyzes and extracts information from a humorous narrative to answer literal, inferential, and applied questions
- Makes predictions about a narrative and uses these to plan a role-play

---

ANSWER KEY

Literal (Page 16)

1. They were playing a type of video game in which they raced Formula 1® cars through the streets of Japan.

2. The last time she babysat them, Meg fell asleep on the couch.

3. Scott was given a fairy costume to wear and Kate the wrestler's costume; they had assumed it would be the other way around.

Inferential (Page 16)

1. No, Meg did not need the photographs for a web page. Include one of the following to support your claim:

   - The company Meg is creating a website for is called "Brats Costumes and Accessories." She was referring to the previous behavior of the children.

   - Meg had a mischievous smile when she was taking her digital camera from her bag.

2. Answers will vary. Possible answer(s): mad; angry; vengeful; she may have reacted by yelling, "Why, those brats!"; her mouth may have dropped to the ground out of astonishment.

3. The text mentions that the kids are going to get away with their antics once again.

Applied (Page 17)

1–4. Answers will vary.

Applying Strategies (Page 18)

1–3. Answers will vary.

EXTENSIONS

- Other humorous books students may enjoy include the following:
  - *Paul Jennings' Funniest Stories* by Paul Jennings
  - *The Giraffe and the Pelly and Me* by Roald Dahl
  - *The 26-Story Treehouse* by Andy Griffiths

Name _____

Read the humorous narrative and answer the questions on the following pages.

"Meg! Thanks so much for coming. I'll be home before midnight. Have fun, kids!" Their mother skips out the front door, her car keys jingling in her hand.

Only moments before, Kate and Scott had been sitting on the carpet in front of the television, laughing and cheering as they raced their Formula 1® cars through the streets of Japan. When the doorbell rang, both cars had spun out of control and crashed.

Now the siblings are frozen in place and silent, staring up at the woman standing in their doorway. Kate and Scott gulp in unison as they think back to how delighted they had been a month ago when they slipped out of their bedrooms to discover Meg, their babysitter, asleep on the couch.

The children had thought it would be hilarious to "borrow" Meg's lipstick from her purse and put it on Ralph, their Rottweiler—returning it with dog hair and slobber on it. Scott had thought it ingenious to empty out Meg's perfume bottle and fill it with water from the toilet. Meanwhile, Kate was emptying out Meg's tub of hair gel, replacing it with cleaning product from under the laundry sink.

Suddenly, Meg speaks, making both children jump. "Let's make a deal, kids. You do a favor for me, and I won't tell your mother about the pranks you pulled when I was 'resting my eyes' the last time I babysat you."

Kate and Scott begin nodding frantically, and slight, wry grins appear on their faces as they realize that, once again, they are going to get away with their antics.

"You see . . . during the day I work as a web designer." As both children look confused, Meg explains further. "Companies ask me to design websites for them. I'm creating one for a company called 'Brats Costumes and Accessories,' and I need some pictures of kids in these costumes for a web page."

Meg takes a pink, sparkling fairy costume and a blue and red spandex wrestler's costume out of a paper bag. The children's grins broaden as they realize that the evening is going to be a lot more fun than they had first expected. That is until Meg hands Scott the fairy costume and Kate the wrestling costume. Meg turns away—hiding her mischievous smile from the pair—and takes the digital camera from her bag.

The next day at school, Kate and Scott are sitting at their desks in their separate classrooms. The bell to start the day rings, and as they always do, their teachers walk over to the classroom computers and turn them on. Today though, the school's web page doesn't appear on the screen. Instead, pictures of Kate and Scott in their costumes are fading in and out to the sounds of some loud, and rather embarrassing, sound effects. The children's classmates notice immediately and run over to the computers. Their laughter begins as small chuckles and grows into hysterical fits. In both classrooms, Kate and Scott are trying desperately to disappear underneath their desks.

THE BABYSITTER'S REVENGE

Literal   Find the answers directly in the text.

1. What were Kate and Scott doing before they realized they were being babysat by Meg?

_____

_____

2. Why were the children able to play pranks on Meg the last time she babysat them?

_____

_____

3. Why were Scott and Kate surprised when they were given the costumes to wear?

_____

_____

Inferential   Think about what the text says.

1. Do you think Meg needed the photographs for a web page she was designing? Look for a clue in the text that tells you she may have been lying.

_____

_____

2. Write some words and phrases to describe how you think Meg reacted and felt when she discovered that the contents of her purse had been tampered with.

_____

_____

3. Do you think that Kate and Scott are normally well-behaved children? Explain your answer.

_____

_____

THE BABYSITTER'S REVENGE

Use what you know about the text and your own experience.

1. Do you think Meg will agree to babysit the children again? Explain your answer.

_____
_____
_____
_____

2. Do you think the children deserved to be humiliated in front of their friends? Explain your answer.

_____
_____
_____
_____
_____

3. If you were Meg, what would have been a better way to handle the situation?

_____
_____
_____
_____

4. Should Meg get in trouble for the prank she pulled? Why or why not?

_____
_____
_____
_____

THE BABYSITTER'S REVENGE

Kate, Scott, and their mother have been called into the principal's office to explain how and why their images now appear on the school's website.

1. **a.** In groups of four, allocate a character to each person in your group.

    Kate: _____   The children's mother: _____

    Scott: _____   The principal: _____

    b. Discuss the situation with your group. Make some predictions about what each of the characters would be thinking and saying about the incident.

The Principal	The Children's Mother
Kate	**Scott**

2. Plan and present a humorous role-play that takes place in the principal's office.

    a. How does the scene start? _____

    _____

    b. How do Scott and Kate explain their images on the school's website? _____

    _____

    c. How does the scene end? _____

    _____

3. Practice your role-play. When you are ready, present it to the class.

Genre: Fable

READING FOCUS

- Analyzes and extracts information from a fable to answer literal, inferential, and applied questions
- Scans a text for information to create a new text, written from one character's point of view
- Predicts future events in a fictional text from a character's point of view

ANSWER KEY

Literal (Page 21)

1.

Who?	What did they demand?
Women	Someone to ride the donkey
Old man	The father to ride the donkey
Girls	The son to ride the donkey
Travelers	No one should ride the donkey

2. A group of girls had scolded him for riding the donkey while his son walked beside him like a servant. He was embarrassed.

Inferential (Page 21)

1. c—He who tries to please everybody, pleases nobody.

2. Answers will vary.

Applied (Page 22)

1. Answers will vary.

2. a–b. Answers will vary.

3. It's not a good idea to try to please everyone because it's impossible to please everybody. Everyone has their own likes and dislikes.

Applying Strategies (Page 23)

Answers will vary.

EXTENSIONS

- Anthologies of Aesop's fables can be found in collections in the library or on the Internet.
- Read more of Aesop's fables:
  - "The Grasshopper and the Ant"
  - "The Tortoise and the Hare"
  - "The Boy Who Cried Wolf"
  - "The Lion and the Mouse"

THE FARMER, HIS SON, AND A DONKEY

Name _____

Read the fable and answer the questions on the following pages.

A farmer stood shaking his head after inspecting his meager wheat crop. He concluded that it would not support his family for the following year, so he called for his son to prepare the donkey to be sold at the markets.

The farmer, the son, and the donkey walked side by side to the market. On their journey, they passed a group of women who started to laugh when they saw the trio.

"Why are you both walking beside a donkey when you could ride it?" they asked curiously.

The farmer shrugged and ordered his son to climb up on the donkey's back. They continued along the path to the market until they passed an old man who pointed his finger at them in anger.

"You ungrateful boy! Why do you ride like a king when your poor father walks on his tired feet? Children have lost all respect for their elders!" the old man scolded.

The farmer looked at his son, who slid down the side of the donkey—his face red with shame. The father shrugged again and mounted the donkey's back.

Moments later, they walked past a group of young girls who were astonished at the sight before them.

"You are a cruel man," the girls jeered. "Why do you ride while your son stumbles along beside you like a servant?"

The boy looked up at his father, whose face was beet-red. The farmer motioned for the donkey to stop so that his son could climb aboard.

Just outside the village, a group of travelers were sitting by a small fire having a conversation. When they saw the two passengers on the donkey, they stopped chatting and called out in anger.

"Why do you ride that poor donkey? Can you not see his back buckling under your weight? It would be smarter for you to carry him than he to carry you!"

The boy and his father quickly dismounted the donkey and looked for a long pole. They tied the donkey's legs together, attached him upside down to the pole, and then positioned the pole on their shoulders.

As they entered the market, the donkey, seeing the market stalls and villagers upside down, decided he was not happy with his predicament and began to kick and buck so hard that the ropes broke, and he fell to the ground. In an instant, the donkey had galloped away. The farmer and his son stood and watched in amazement as the donkey disappeared from their sight.

THE FARMER, HIS SON, AND A DONKEY

Literal   Find the answers directly in the text.

1. Complete the chart.

Who?	What did they demand?
	Someone to ride the donkey
Old man	
	Son to ride the donkey
Travelers	

2. What caused the farmer's face to turn beet-red?

_____

_____

Inferential   Think about what the text says.

1. A fable is a story that teaches the reader a lesson about how to behave. The lesson is what's called the "moral" of the story. What do you think the moral of this fable is?

   a. ☐ Slow and steady wins the race.

   b. ☐ It is easier to think up a plan than to carry it out.

   c. ☐ He who tries to please everybody, pleases nobody.

2. Explain your choice.

_____

_____

_____

THE FARMER, HIS SON, AND A DONKEY

Applied   Use what you know about the text and your own experience.

1. **"It would be smarter for you to carry him than he to carry you!"**

   Do you think the travelers meant for the farmer and the son to carry the donkey? Explain your answer.

   _____

   _____

   _____

2. **a.** Who do you think had the right idea about the trip to the markets?

   ☐ Farmer and son   ☐ Women   ☐ Old man   ☐ Girls   ☐ Travelers

   b. Explain your choice.

   _____

   _____

   _____

   _____

3. Why is it not a good idea to try and please everyone?

   _____

   _____

   _____

   _____

   _____

   _____

   _____

THE FARMER, HIS SON, AND A DONKEY

Use the text on page 20 to complete the activities. Retell the story of the trio's journey to the markets from the donkey's point of view. Include what the donkey was thinking during the day's events and reveal what happened to him once he had fled the markets.

Your story can be in the form of: ☐ a diary   ☐ a play   ☐ a narrative story (with dialogue)

Title: _____

What were you thinking when you left the farm?	_____

_____

_____

| | Who did you meet along the way? |

| How did you feel about your passengers? | _____ |

_____

_____

| Where did you run to? | _____ |

_____

| | Who did you meet there? |

_____

_____

Unit 4
Sarah and the Secret Castle

Genre: Fairy Tale

READING FOCUS

- Analyzes and extracts information from a modern-day fairy tale to answer literal, inferential, and applied questions
- Makes connections between himself/herself and a character from a fictional text
- Predicts future events in a fictional text from a character's point of view

ANSWER KEY

Literal (Page 26)

1. a. a very best friend.

   b. she spotted the long silver car Josephine disappeared into at the end of each school day outside a shabby gray apartment building.

   c. exist behind the front door of a shabby gray apartment building.

2. Three of the following:

   - the butler
   - magnificent ballroom with chandeliers, marble floor, and statues
   - servants dusting and polishing
   - Josephine's lavender ball gown and tiara

Inferential (Page 26)

1. Answers will vary. Possible answer(s): uneasy, anxious, nervous, a little embarrassed, wants to be like the other students.

2. Answers will vary. Possible answer(s): Josephine doesn't want others to treat her differently, she doesn't want all the attention, she wants to be an ordinary girl.

Applied (Page 27)

1–3. Answers will vary.

4. Drawings will vary.

Applying Strategies (Page 28)

1–2. Answers will vary.

EXTENSIONS

- Read other fairy tales and fractured fairy tales, such as:
  - *Snow White in New York* by Fiona French
  - *Princess Smartypants* by Babette Cole
  - *The Paper Bag Princess* by Robert Munsch
  - *Revolting Rhymes* by Roald Dahl
  - *Legally Correct Fairy Tales* by David Fisher

SARAH AND THE SECRET CASTLE

Name _____

Read the modern-day fairy tale and answer the questions on the following pages.

Once upon a time, there lived two girls who were in the same class at school. Sarah was quite boisterous and was always telling jokes that made her classmates laugh. Josephine was quiet, well-mannered, and elegant. Most lunchtimes, both girls could be found on the playground. Josephine would gracefully sit on the swings, while Sarah would swing across the monkey bars with ease.

Looking from the outside, the two girls had very little in common. However, there was one thing that they did share—a secret wish to have a very best friend.

One afternoon, Sarah was walking home from her guitar lesson when she spotted the long silver car Josephine disappeared into at the end of each school day. It was parked outside a shabby gray apartment building. Sarah decided she would see if Josephine wanted to play with her. She tapped on the closest door, which was quickly opened by a tall, distinguished looking man. He was wearing a white shirt with a winged collar and tie, a black coat with tails, and pinstriped trousers. The man instantly frowned.

"Please go away!" he snapped at Sarah. "Do not come here again."

Sarah stared at what she guessed was Josephine's butler. Being the rascal that she was, Sarah ducked down and scrambled into the house through the butler's legs. She quickly stood up and was about to make a run for it to find Josephine, but instead she froze on the spot! Before her was a magnificent grand ballroom—the size of her school hall! Sarah did a double-take, looking back at the front door and then again at the enormous room. It had many chandeliers hanging from its high ceiling, a pristine marble floor, and amazing statues that servants were busily dusting and polishing.

Sarah spotted an elegant girl walking down a staircase, wearing a spectacular lavender ball gown. Her hair was piled on top of her head and featured a sparkling tiara.

"You're a princess!" Sarah called out to Josephine, who spun around in her dainty white shoes. Josephine glided over to Sarah and gently pushed her through a marble archway into a room with a dining table the length of a swimming pool!

"How did you . . ." Josephine began. But then she shook her head and started to whisper. "You are right. I am a princess. This is my family's castle. You HAVE to promise not to tell. You MUST promise!"

A mischievous smirk spread across Sarah's face. Although her mind was spinning with questions about how a castle could exist behind the front door of a shabby gray apartment, Sarah remembered her secret wish.

"I promise I won't tell . . . but only if you let me play here in the castle with you."

"OK!" Josephine giggled with excitement, remembering a little too late to politely cover her mouth. "If you think this room is amazing, wait until you see my bedroom! Oh! And the stables—they're full of ponies!"

Princess Josephine and Sarah made a pact to spend every Saturday afternoon playing together in the castle. And this is exactly what they did. Not long after that, they became the very best of friends.

SARAH AND THE SECRET CASTLE

Literal   Find the answers directly in the text.

1. Complete these sentences.

    a. Both girls secretly wished they had _____.

    b. Sarah discovered where Josephine lived because _____

    _____.

    c. Sarah was confused about how a castle could _____

    _____.

2. List three things that helped Sarah determine that Josephine was a princess.

    • _____

    • _____

    • _____

Inferential   Think about what the text says.

1. Write words and phrases to describe how you think Josephine may have felt having to pretend to her classmates that she was an ordinary girl.

    _____

    _____

    _____

2. Why do you think Josephine made Sarah promise that she wouldn't tell her secret?

    _____

    _____

    _____

SARAH AND THE SECRET CASTLE

Applied   Use what you know about the text and your own experience.

1. Do you think Sarah kept her promise? Explain your answer.

   _____

   _____

   _____

   _____

2. Which character from the story do you relate to the most? Place an **X** next to the traits you have.

   Sarah: ☐ joker   ☐ boisterous   ☐ athletic   ☐ mischievous

   Josephine: ☐ graceful   ☐ polite   ☐ quiet   ☐ proud

3. Imagine another student had approached Sarah speculating about Josephine being a princess. If you were Sarah, how would you handle the suspicion?

   _____

   _____

   _____

   _____

4. Draw what you think the inside of the castle looked like.

SARAH AND THE SECRET CASTLE

Making Connections

Use the text on page 25 to help you complete the following activity.

1. **a.** Sarah had so many questions to ask her new best friend. Write four questions you think she might have asked Princess Josephine.

    - _____
    - _____
    - _____
    - _____

    b. Circle one of the questions. Answer it as if you were Princess Josephine.

    _____

    _____

2. Sarah and Princess Josephine spent so many Saturday afternoons playing together that Sarah's mischievous personality began to influence her new best friend. Choose one of the characters, and write a diary entry that describes a Saturday afternoon's adventure.

    Predicting

    Character: ☐ Princess Josephine ☐ Sarah

    Saturday _____

    _____

    _____

    _____

    _____

    _____

    _____

    _____

    _____

Genre: Fantasy

READING FOCUS

- Analyzes and extracts information from a fantasy to answer literal, inferential, and applied questions
- Synthesizes information from a text to create a diary of a character
- Makes connections between a character in a text and himself/herself to write a personal diary

ANSWER KEY

Literal (Page 31)

1. Peril Sands
2. Sanzoc, a Sand Creature from the Dodzin Desert
3. Flying Ferriers
4. Desert Dopplers
5. Sashoc, the great-granddaughter of Sanzoc

Inferential (Page 31)

1. The competitors are lucky because the falling boulders could do more damage, but luckily, it just knocks them unconscious; they are lucky that the head trauma didn't end their lives.
2. Answers will vary. Possible answer(s): nervous, anxious, eager, proud, stressed, weight of the world on her shoulders, scared, worried.
3. The spectators are excited and looking forward to the Great Race, but in the back of their minds they wish that life after the race could be without war and be peaceful.

Applied (Page 32)

1. Answers will vary. Possible answer(s): She didn't have a choice because the entire race of Sand Creatures is depending on her to win the race; she was born in a family of Racers; or she had the choice because people would understand that she was young; she could have decided on her own to save the Sand Creature population.
2. Answers will vary.
3. Answers will vary.

Applying Strategies (Page 33)

Answers will vary.

EXTENSIONS

- Students can read other novels that are set in nonexistent worlds, such as:
  - *The Hobbit* by J.R.R. Tolkien
  - *The Golden Compass* by Philip Pullman
  - *Harry Potter* series by J.K. Rowling
  - *The Neverending Story* by Michael Ende

Name _____

Read the fantasy story and answer the questions on the following pages.

Creatures from all over Namboodya have camped out under the Great Star and seven moons, excitedly anticipating the Great Race. It is the highlight of the year for all who inhabit Namboodya. For on this one day, as it has been for hundreds of centuries, all wars cease and all conflicts are put aside.

Peril Sands, the barren stretch of land between the Areill Mountains and the town of Nambi, is the site for the race. Once the moons have disappeared over the mountains, the spectators dash toward either side of the stretch of sand, vying for good positions. The diversity of creatures gathered at Peril Sands is spectacular. All unite here, noisily cheering on the competitors, but silently they wish, most of all, that the peace will remain.

In the history of the Great Race, only one has made it to the finish line unhurt. Sanzoc, a Sand Creature from the Dodzin Desert, was born into a family of Racers. He trained his entire life for the Race and altered Namboodya's history when he won it. Arriving at the finish line first, and with no injuries, earned him the title of the Great Race Champion. His statue marks the finish line.

Today, 14 Racers wait in grand tents filled with servants and gifts. Their family members parade into the tents to wish them luck and godspeed. The Racers not only have to travel the long distance to the finish line, they must also avoid treacherous obstacles. One of these are the Sand Suckers—little pockets in the sand that viciously suck at random. Any creature unfortunate enough to be standing on a Sand Sucker when it decides to suck, is lost to the sands forever.

The second hurdle the Racers face are the Flying Ferriers. These winged, dog-like creatures inhabit the skies of Peril Sands. They swoop down and pick up large rocks in their mouths, dropping them to the ground when they become too heavy. The lucky competitors are only knocked unconscious by the falling boulders.

The 15th Racer in the competition sits alone in a plain tent of modest size, waiting for the sounds of the horns to announce the start of the race. Sashoc is a Sand Creature from the Dodzin Desert and the youngest of the competitors. She is also the great-granddaughter of Sanzoc.

Sashoc nervously chews on her nails. Her whole village, indeed the entire race of Sand Creatures, is depending on her to win the race. The winner is given the privilege of stopping one of the many wars across the land of Namboodya. As her people will not survive another year of trying to prevent the vicious Desert Dopplers from taking their land, Sashoc must win!

The horns sound, alerting the thousands of spectators that the race is about to begin. Their cheers are deafening. Sashoc stands, clenching and unclenching her hands. She takes a deep breath and exhales slowly, sweeping aside the flap at the entrance to her tent.

THE GREAT RACE

Literal   Find the answers directly in the text.

1. Name the place where the Great Race is held.

   _____

2. Name the Great Race Champion.

   _____

3. Name the winged, dog-like creatures who inhabit the skies.

   _____

4. Name the enemy of the Sand Creatures.

   _____

5. Name the youngest competitor in the Great Race.

   _____

Inferential   Think about what the text says.

1. The Flying Ferriers drop rocks from the skies onto the competitors. Why are the competitors who are "only knocked unconscious" lucky?

   _____

   _____

2. List some words and phrases to describe how you think Sashoc must be feeling before the Great Race.

   _____

   _____

3. **All unite here, noisily cheering on the competitors, but silently they wish, most of all, that the peace will remain.**

   What does this sentence from the text mean?

   _____

   _____

THE GREAT RACE

Applied   Use what you know about the text and your own experience.

1. Do you think that Sashoc, being the great-granddaughter of Sanzoc, had a choice about becoming a Racer? Explain your answer.

_____

_____

_____

_____

2. Would you like to live in the land of Namboodya? Explain your answer.

_____

_____

_____

_____

3. If you were Sachoc, what would be some thoughts going through your mind? Write down some phrases you would say to yourself.

_____

_____

_____

_____

_____

_____

_____

_____

_____

THE GREAT RACE

Use the text on page 30 to complete the activities. You are Sashoc and it is a week before the Great Race.

Complete your personal diary for the week, including details such as:

- everyday elements of your life, such as where you live, what you eat, and how you are affected by the war with the Desert Dopplers.

- your training regime so that you will be prepared for the Sand Suckers and Flying Ferriers.

- traveling to and arriving at Peril Sands.

> *5 days until the Great Race.*
>
> *Today I...* _____
>
> _____
>
> _____
>
> *4 days to go!* _____
>
> _____
>
> _____
>
> *3 days until the race!* _____
>
> _____
>
> _____
>
> *2 days left!* _____
>
> _____
>
> _____
>
> *Tomorrow is the Great Race. Today, I must...* _____
>
> _____
>
> _____
>
> _____
>
> _____

Genre: Mystery

READING FOCUS

- Analyzes and extracts information from a mystery narrative to answer literal, inferential, and applied questions
- Makes connections between himself/herself and a character from a fictional text
- Summarizes the events in a fictional text from a character's point of view

ANSWER KEY

Literal (Page 36)

1. He was out of work.

2. a. the sun shimmering on the dolphin's skin was very bright

   b. dug/scrabbled; a leather sack full of gold coins

   c. gray, silky clothes; the tail of a dolphin

Inferential (Page 36)

1. a. Answers will vary. Possible answer(s): surprised, nervous, scared, astonished, flabbergasted, amazed, stunned, shocked, dumbfounded.

   b. Answers will vary. Possible answer(s): bewildered, confused, puzzled, mystified, baffled, curious.

2. Answers will vary. Possible answer(s): Hamish was in shock and couldn't process what he was seeing; he could have been scared.

Applied (Page 37)

1. a–b. Answers will vary.

2. a. Answers will vary. Possible answer(s): they can worry less about their dad being out of work, they'll have money to go on nicer vacations, their family will have the money to pay for things they need.

   b. Answers will vary.

Applying Strategies (Page 38)

1–3. Answers will vary.

EXTENSIONS

- Read other mystery tales, such as:
  - *Antonio S and the Mystery of Theodore Guzman* by Odo Hirsch
  - *Emily Eyefinger* series by Duncan Ball
  - *Encyclopedia Brown* series by Donald J. Sobol
  - *The Roman Mysteries* series by Caroline Lawrence

THE DOLPHIN MYSTERY

Name _____

Read the mystery story and answer the questions on the following pages.

"This is the worst vacation I've ever been on," Hamish sighed, kicking at the sand.

Ingrid nodded. "It was nice of Uncle Ray to let us stay at his beach house. But I can't stop thinking about Dad being out of work. There's going to be very little money around for a while." She bit her lip and felt for her dolphin necklace. She had bought it at the fair that morning with her last bit of pocket money, from a gypsy woman with black, liquid eyes. It wasn't the sort of jewelry Ingrid normally liked, but somehow the woman had made her feel that she just had to own it.

"Look at that!"

Ingrid glanced up and saw Hamish pointing out to sea. There was a dolphin, swimming straight toward them. Ingrid scrambled to her feet and waded into the water. To her surprise, the dolphin glided up to her, its head bumping against her legs. Its skin was shimmering in the sun so brightly that Ingrid shut her eyes. Then, she heard Hamish gasp and she opened her eyes again. Her heart skipped a beat. The dolphin had vanished, and in its place was a woman with gray, silky clothes and long, tangled hair.

Ingrid shivered. "Who . . . who are you?"

The woman uttered soft squeaks and clicks. Her gaze was fixed on something behind Ingrid.

"Do you w-want to go up there?" asked Ingrid. Her mouth was dry.

The woman nodded and looked down at the water. Ingrid could see that she didn't have legs or feet—she had the tail of a dolphin.

"We have to help her," said Ingrid. She prodded her brother, who seemed to be frozen in place. "Come on, Hamish."

Ingrid put her arm around the woman's waist and waited for Hamish to do the same. She braced her muscles for a heavy weight, but the woman was surprisingly light. Ingrid and Hamish dragged her over the seaweed and up the deserted beach. Suddenly, she began to squeak excitedly, pointing at the sand.

"I don't understand," said Ingrid. She looked into the woman's black, liquid eyes.

"She wants us to dig," said Hamish. "Don't you?"

The woman nodded. She wriggled, and Hamish and Ingrid set her gently on the ground. Hamish crouched down and scrabbled in the sand, but Ingrid stared at the woman. Who was she? What did she want? Ingrid knew she ought to feel scared, but instead she was filled with a sense of calm.

"There's something here!" Hamish said. He reached into the hole he'd made and pulled up a leather sack. Ingrid held her breath as her brother untied the silk cord. Ingrid's mouth fell open. The sack was full of gold coins.

"We're rich!" yelled Hamish. He scooped up some of the coins and threw them into the air, whooping for joy. Then, he stared past Ingrid. "She's gone," he said.

Ingrid whipped her head around and then jumped to her feet, scanning the sea. A dolphin was leaping in the air, far in the distance. Ingrid felt for her necklace and swallowed. What had happened? She had to go back to the fair to find out.

Name _____

THE DOLPHIN MYSTERY

Activities

Literal Find the answers directly in the text.

1. What had happened to Ingrid and Hamish's dad?

   _____

   _____

2. Complete these sentences.

   a. Ingrid shut her eyes because _____

      _____.

   b. Hamish _____ in the sand

      and found _____.

   c. The woman was wearing _____

      and had _____ instead of legs and feet.

Inferential Think about what the text says.

1. List words to describe how Ingrid may have felt when:

   a. she first saw the woman in the water.

      _____

   b. she saw the dolphin leaping in the air.

      _____

2. Why do you think Hamish was "frozen in place"?

   _____

   _____

   _____

#8248 Comprehending Text   36   ©Teacher Created Resources

THE DOLPHIN MYSTERY

Applied   Use what you know about the text and your own experience.

1.   **a.** If you were Ingrid, what would you have done with the dolphin necklace until you got back to the fair?

☐ kept wearing it   ☐ thrown it away   ☐ put it in your pocket

☐ other _____

   b. Write reasons for your answer.

_____

_____

_____

_____

2.   **a.** In what ways will their life change now that they have a sack full of gold coins?

_____

_____

_____

_____

   b. What would you do with a sack full of gold coins?

_____

_____

_____

_____

THE DOLPHIN MYSTERY

Summarizing   Use the text on page 35 to help you summarize the events
from Ingrid's point of view.

1. Imagine you are Ingrid. Complete a diary entry that summarizes the events of the day described in the
story. Use the facts that are given as well as your own ideas.

> *Dear Diary,*
>
> *This morning, I went to the fair . . .*
>
>
>
> *This afternoon, Hamish and I went to the beach . . .*

2. Ingrid has decided to go back to the fair to talk to the gypsy woman.
Write three questions you think she should ask the gypsy woman to help
her solve the mystery.

Making Connections

- _____

- _____

- _____

3. Choose one of your questions from question #2. Answer it as if you were the gypsy woman. You can
be as mysterious as you like.

_____

_____

_____

Genre: **Adventure**

READING FOCUS

- Analyzes and extracts information from an adventure story to answer literal, inferential, and applied questions
- Makes a connection between the actions of a character in a text and himself/herself

ANSWER KEY

Literal (Page 41)

1. tin box, trees, ducks
2. Maddy's pigtails were lopsided.
3. small cars, toy soldiers, sports cards, and old coins

Inferential (Page 41)

1. Maddy is most likely the youngest.

   Sentence copied will vary but should be evidence that supports Maddy being the youngest.

2. Ryan is the leader of the expedition.

   Sentence copied will vary but should be evidence that Ryan was the one giving orders and leading the way.

Applied (Page 42)

1.

Story Genre—adventure	Title—*Bowey Island*
Characters—Ryan, Sam, and Maddy	
Setting—Bowey Island	
Events and Actions—The children rowed across the lake to Bowey Island. While on their walk, a branch caught hold of one of Maddy's pigtails. Sam freed her from the tree and realized that it was the tree they were looking for. They followed the map and walked the number of paces the map showed. Ryan and Sam dug near the water's edge. Sam found an old tin box. Inside were their father's little treasures that he had buried when he was a boy.	

2. Drawings will vary but should show the right amount of paces.

Applying Strategies (Page 43)

1–2. Answers/drawings will vary.

EXTENSIONS

- Students can write the next chapter of the story, choosing one of the following events:
  - The children return to their boat to discover that the oars have drifted away across the lake.
  - While the boys are looking at the contents of the tin, Maddy wanders away and encounters a snake.
  - On the journey back, Sam falls out of the boat and begins to panic in the cold water.

Name _____

Read the chapter from an adventure novel and answer the questions on the following pages.

CHAPTER 4

The children collected the old boat from their grandfather's old shed, as they did at the beginning of every summer vacation. But this time they weren't rowing across the lake to Bowey Island to catch fish, or set up a tent, or go swimming. This expedition had a purpose. They wanted to see if the map Ryan had found slipped inside a book in their grandparents' bookshelf was authentic.

"Put your life jacket on, Maddy," Ryan ordered. "Sam, push us off!"

The children set off from the wooden jetty on their grandparent's property. Maddy sat in the bow, looking tiny in her bright yellow life jacket. Because she wasn't used to doing her own hair, her pigtails were lopsided, making her look as though she might tip over at any minute.

After a silent trip (apart from the occasional grunt from Ryan struggling with the oars), the children arrived at the island.

"OK! The map says we have to find the tree with the largest trunk and stand facing the Bowey Estate," called Ryan.

Ryan walked quickly between the trees and bushes, dodging the sharp branches and prickly leaves. Maddy tried to follow her brother, but a branch caught hold of one of her pigtails, causing her to yelp.

Sam caught up with his sister, and while he was untangling her from the tree's grasp, he realized that this was the tree they had been searching for. Ryan joined the pair and stood where he could see their grandparents' house through the bushes and trees.

"We need to walk ten paces and turn east. Hmmm . . . I wonder if that's east for real or east from the direction we are facing?" Ryan speculated. He decided to turn east from the house and step out the paces. Maddy and Sam followed him.

"OK! Now we must walk 13 paces and turn south and then another 11 paces. If we have followed the map correctly, then that is where we should dig."

Maddy held up her miniature garden shovel that she had taken from the shed.

The children stepped out the number of paces and arrived at an area not far from the water's edge. Sam pointed out the duck prints in the mud.

Ryan and Sam began digging with their hands—scooping out the dirt into small piles. Maddy, crouched down by the site, clapped excitedly.

"I've found something!" Sam exclaimed. "It feels like a tin."

The boys retrieved an old tin box from the ground and opened it. Inside was a menagerie of little treasures—small cars, toy soldiers, some type of sports cards, and old coins. It wasn't long before they realized that these were their father's things that he must have buried when he was a boy.

"Wait until we show these to Dad! I bet he has forgotten all about them!" said Sam, smiling.

BOWEY ISLAND

Literal   Find the answers directly in the text.

1. Place an **X** next to the three things that are on Bowey Island.

   ☐ jetty   ☐ tin box   ☐ trees   ☐ house   ☐ ducks   ☐ old shed

2. Why does Maddy look as though she is about to tip over?

   _____

   _____

3. What four things are discovered in the tin box dug up on the island?

   • _____

   • _____

   • _____

   • _____

Inferential   Think about what the text says.

1. Who is most likely the youngest of the three siblings? _____

   Copy a sentence from the text that helped you to decide this.

   _____

   _____

   _____

2. Who do you think is the leader of the expedition across the lake to the island? _____

   Copy a sentence from the text that helped you to decide this.

   _____

   _____

   _____

Name _____

Name _____

BOWEY ISLAND

Applied Use what you know about the text and your own experience.

1. Complete the table about the adventure story *Bowey Island*.

Story Genre		Title
Characters		
Setting		
Events and Actions		

2. Draw what the map looked like based on the descriptions from the text.

Name _____

BOWEY ISLAND

Making Connections

When the children's father was a boy, he collected his most prized possessions, placed them in a tin, and buried them on Bowey Island. He was creating a time capsule that contained what was important to him at the time.

1. Imagine you are going to create a time capsule and bury four of your most treasured items in it. What would they be, and why would you choose them?

My first item would be _____
because _____
_____
_____.

My second item would be _____
because _____
_____
_____.

My third item would be _____
because _____
_____
_____.

My fourth item would be _____
because _____
_____
_____.

2. **a.** Where would you bury your time capsule?

   _____
   _____
   _____

   b. In the space provided, draw a map of where you would bury your time capsule.

Genre: Persuasive

READING FOCUS

- Analyzes and extracts information from persuasive texts to answer literal, inferential, and applied questions
- Makes comparisons between two persuasive texts
- Synthesizes information about the conventions of persuasive texts to write a letter

ANSWER KEY

Literal (Page 46)

Letter 1 three of the following:

- seating causes splinters
- seating has no back support
- painful for parents to sit as they watch children play sports for hours
- could cause permanent back injury

Letter 2

- destroying native plants
- increasing effects of erosion
- dunes won't be there for grandchildren to see

Inferential (Page 46)

1. Letter 1—three of the following: like to appeal, we urge, it is essential, surely

   Letter 2—three of the following: inform, I shudder to think, the effects of, lost forever, do we want our grandchildren and their children, implore, before it is too late, must protect

2. a. Letter 1

   b. "Currently, the seating is a not-so-'grand' stand of rough wooden planks that deliver cruel splinters to anyone who sits on them."

Applied (Page 47)

1–3. Answers will vary.

Applying Strategies (Page 48)

1–2. Answers will vary.

EXTENSIONS

- Students can study text that has been read in class and collect and investigate words that are used to persuade the reader. For example, rhetorical questions and keywords and phrases that encourage the reader to accept a point of view, such as, "surely," "moreover," "because," etc.
- Students can look in newspapers at the "Letters to the Editor" section and underline persuasive words and phrases.

Name _____

Read the persuasive texts and answer the questions on the following pages.

BAKERSTOWN COUNCIL – Letter 1
Re: Seating at Bakerstown Sports Stadium

To whom it may concern,

We would like to appeal to the Council for an urgent upgrade of the seating at the Bakerstown Sports Stadium. Currently, the seating is a not-so-"grand" stand of rough wooden planks that deliver cruel splinters to anyone who sits on them.

The planks have nothing to support a person's back and become excruciatingly uncomfortable to sit on after several hours of watching a game.

As we refuse to abandon our children during their moments of glory on the playing fields, we urge the Council to consider the parents of this town who suffer the misfortune and agony of having to spend their Saturdays on the seating at the stadium.

It is essential that this matter be a priority for the Council before permanent back injury is caused to a spectator by the seating at the Bakerstown Sports Stadium. Surely it would be cheaper to upgrade the seating than pay medical expenses for injured spectators, wouldn't it?

—Karen O'Brien
 Parents Committee of Bakerstown Little League

BAKERSTOWN COUNCIL – Letter 2
Re: Baker's Beach Sand Dunes

To whom it may concern,

I am writing to inform the Council of the tragedy that occurs every summer at Baker's Beach.

Beachgoers appear oblivious to the damage they are causing to the Baker's Beach sand dunes when they ignore the path from the parking lot to the ocean and instead, trudge through the dunes.

I shudder to think that with another summer approaching, kids will be sliding down the dunes on their boogie boards, crushing native plants and leaving the dunes bare and vulnerable. The effects of erosion will increase, and the sand will be blown away and lost forever!

Do we want our grandchildren and their children to only be able to witness the beauty of the Baker's Beach sand dunes as photographs in books?

I implore the Council to construct a fence around the dunes and create warning signs to educate people about the consequences of their destructive behavior before it is too late. We must protect our natural environment!

—Jeff Baker
 Bakerstown Coastal Care Organization

BAKERSTOWN COUNCIL

Literal   Find the answers directly in the text.

Find three reasons in each letter that states why the Council should agree to what is being asked.

Letter 1	**Letter 2**
• _____	• _____
• _____	• _____
• _____	• _____

Inferential   Think about what the text says.

1. Choose three words or phrases from each letter that you think may help to persuade the Council; for example, "surely."

Letter 1	**Letter 2**
• _____	• _____
• _____	• _____
• _____	• _____

2. **a.** Which letter has a hint of sarcasm? _____

    b. Copy a sentence from the letter that demonstrates sarcasm.

_____

_____

_____

Name _____

Activities

BAKERSTOWN COUNCIL

Applied   Use what you know about the text and your own experience.

1. Mark an **X** next to the name of who you think is more successful at persuading a reader to agree with his/her point of view.

   ☐ Karen O'Brien   ☐ Jeff Baker

   Explain your choice.

   _____

   _____

   _____

   _____

   _____

2. If the Bakerstown Council only has enough money to budget for one of the projects requested in the letters, which project do you think they should choose?

   ☐ Stadium seating   ☐ Sand dunes fencing

   Explain your choice.

   _____

   _____

   _____

   _____

3. What issue around your town would you write to your city council about?

   _____

   _____

   _____

   _____

BAKERSTOWN COUNCIL

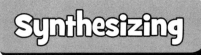

Refer to the texts on page 45 to help you complete these activities. You are a boogie boarder who lives in Bakerstown. Your favorite activity in the summer is sand boarding down the Baker's Beach sand dunes. You have seen flyers stating that the Council is considering putting up a fence around the dunes.

1. Think of three reasons why you want the Council to change its decision about the fence.

- _____
- _____
- _____

2. Write a persuasive letter to the Council that explains why you think it should change its decision about the fence at the Baker's Beach sand dunes.

BAKERSTOWN COUNCIL

Re: Sand Dunes at Baker's Beach

To whom it may concern, _____

Begin with a strong sentence that states your opinion.

Introduce your reasons and give examples.

| Include persuasive words and phrases such as the following:
Surely …
I think that …
You can see that …
Therefore … |
| --- |

Include a rhetorical question to encourage the reader to agree with you.

Finish by repeating your opinion.

Genre: Poetry

READING FOCUS

- Analyzes and extracts information from a poem to answer literal, inferential, and applied questions
- Makes comparisons between two poems
- Scans a poem for relevant information
- Makes connections between feelings expressed in a poem and his/her own feelings

ANSWER KEY

Literal (Page 51)
1. He would like to have a chat with a child and gain a friend.
2. a. sneering, teasing   b. den   c. different   d. toes, noses
3. hurl, shove, spit out, stab

Inferential (Page 51)
1. Answers should indicate that they are harsh-sounding words.
2. Answers will vary.
3. Answers will vary. Possible answer(s): friendly, lonely.

Applied (Page 52)
1–2. Answers will vary.
3. Answers will vary. Possible answer(s): makes life more interesting, more opportunity to learn different things from different people, people have their own strengths and weaknesses.

Applying Strategies (Page 53)
1. a–b.

	"The Troll"	"Different"
Whose point of view is the poem from?	The troll	The narrator
Does the poem rhyme?	☐ Yes ☑ No	☐ Yes ☑ No
Is it divided into verses?	☑ Yes ☐ No	☐ Yes ☑ No
Does the poem tell a story or describe feelings?	tells a story and describes feelings	describes feelings
Is alliteration used (e.g., "racing rabbits," "dim and dusty room")? If yes, write an example.	☑ Yes ☐ No "luscious leaves," "bright berries," "sour seeds," or "fresh fruit"	☑ Yes ☐ No "sneering smile"
Are any lines repeated? If yes, write an example.	☑ Yes ☐ No "'Stay clear away from the forest," they say.'	☑ Yes ☐ No "So" and "I am different from you."

   c. Answers will vary. Possible answer(s): both narrators are lonely, both could use a friend, both are being wrongly judged.
2–3. Answers will vary.

EXTENSIONS

- The teacher can encourage students to find poems they like and perform them for the class with sound effects and movement.
- Collections of poems for children can be found in the following books:
  - *Walking on Air* by Berlie Doherty
  - *The New Oxford Treasury of Children's Poems* by Michael Harrison and Christopher Stuart-Clark
  - *I Like This Poem: A Collection of Best-Loved Poems Chosen by Children for Other Children* edited by Kaye Webb

Name _____

Read the poems and answer the questions on the following pages.

The Troll

"Stay clear away from the forest," they say.
"The troll will catch you for sure.
He lurks near the lake,
He skulks in the shrubs,
And he hides in the hollows of trees."
"If he catches you, you'll be sorry," they say.
"Boys and girls are his favorite lunch.
He thinks toes are tasty,
Hair is like honey,
And noses are just so nice to nibble."

They say anything to keep children away
From my den so deep in the woods
Where I eat luscious leaves,
Bright berries, sour seeds,
And fresh fruit from the trificka tree.
I just can't believe they say I eat kids.
Why would I want to do that?
I'd love to meet one
And have a chat—
A friend for a lonely old troll.

"Stay clear away from the forest," they say.
"The troll's so ugly you'd faint.
He's nothing like us—
Just leave him alone.
Some things aren't fit to have friends."

Different

I am different from you
So
You hurl teasing words at me
Shove laughter in my face
Spit out lies about me
And stab hard stares in my eyes
All with a sneering smile
That shows your cruel heart
So
I am glad
I am different from you.

THE TROLL/DIFFERENT

Literal   Find the answers directly in the text.

Use the poems to answer the questions.

1. Why does the troll say he would like to meet a child?

    _____

2. Complete these sentences.

    a. The person described in "Different" has a _____ smile

       and uses _____ words.

    b. The troll lives in a _____ in the woods.

    c. The narrator of "Different" is glad to be _____ .

    d. In "The Troll", "they" say the troll likes to eat children's hair, _____ ,

       and _____ .

3. List the four verbs used in "Different" that describe the actions of the person with the sneering smile.

    • _____   • _____

    • _____   • _____

Inferential   Think about what the text says.

1. Why do you think the author of "Different" chose the words he/she used for the poem?

    _____

2. Who do you think "they" are in "The Troll"?

    _____

3. List words you think describe the personality of the troll.

    _____

    _____

THE TROLL/DIFFERENT

Activities

Applied — Use what you know about the text and your own experience.

1. Do you agree that the troll isn't "fit to have friends"? Explain why/why not.

_____

_____

_____

_____

_____

2. What age do you imagine the narrator of "Different" to be?

☐ under 8   ☐ 8–12   ☐ teenager   ☐ adult

Give reasons for your answer.

_____

_____

_____

_____

3. Everyone is different; no two people are exactly alike. What are some positive aspects of being different?

_____

_____

_____

_____

_____

THE TROLL/DIFFERENT

Comparing

Complete the following activities to examine the differences and similarities between "The Troll" and "Different."

1. **a.** Compare the two poems by completing the table.

	The Troll	Different
Whose point of view is the poem from?		
Does the poem rhyme?	☐ Yes ☐ No	☐ Yes ☐ No
Is it divided into verses?	☐ Yes ☐ No	☐ Yes ☐ No
Does the poem tell a story or describe feelings?		
Is alliteration used (e.g., "racing rabbits," "dim and dusty room")? If yes, write an example.	☐ Yes ☐ No	☐ Yes ☐ No
Are any lines repeated? If yes, write an example.	☐ Yes ☐ No	☐ Yes ☐ No

b. Look at the table. Circle the things the poems have in common.

c. Name one other thing you noticed the poems have in common.

_____

2. Which poem did you prefer?　☐ "The Troll"　☐ "Different"

Explain why. _____

_____

3. How did your preferred poem make you feel? Describe another piece of writing or a situation that has also made you feel like this.

_____

_____

_____

Genre: Folktale

READING FOCUS

- Analyzes and extracts information from a folktale to answer literal, inferential, and applied questions
- Uses sensory imaging to describe suitable visual and auditory effects for a movie scene based on a text

---

ANSWER KEY

Literal (Page 56)

1. The men had accidentally tickled his lips with one of the palm leaves.

2. a. 2   b. 1   c. 5   d. 4   e. 3

Inferential (Page 56)

1. Answers should indicate that the giant was pretending to be friendly, hoping to trick the men into moving the boulder.

2. Answers will vary.

Applied (Page 57)

1–2. Answers will vary.

Applying Strategies (Page 58)

1–2. Answers will vary.

EXTENSIONS

- Information about the culture of the island of Rotuma can be found online at: *www.rotuma.net*
- Collections of folktales from around the world can be found in the following books:
  - *Folk Tales and Fables of the World* series by Barbara Hayes and Robert Ingpen
  - *Rich Man, Poor Man, Beggarman, Thief: Folk Tales from Around the World* by Marcus Crouch
  - *The Young Oxford Book of Folk Tales* by Kevin Crossley-Holland

Name _____

Read the folktale from the Pacific Islands and answer the questions on the following pages.

Long ago, on the island of Rotuma, a giant lived in a cave high on a mountain. The villagers were terrified of him because his teeth blazed with fire. He only had to open his mouth or smile to make flames leap out and burn whatever was in front of him.

One day, some of the young men of the village decided they would try to steal the giant's fire. None of the villagers knew how to make fire, but they knew it would be useful. So the men gathered some dried coconut palm leaves and climbed up to the giant's cave. They breathed a sigh of relief when they found him asleep. The men watched him for a while. Every time he exhaled, flames poured out, and every time he inhaled, he sucked the flames back into his mouth.

When the men were ready, they crept toward the giant, holding their palm leaves up to his mouth. The next time the giant breathed out, the leaves caught aflame. Excited, the men tiptoed out of the cave. They hadn't noticed that one of the leaves had tickled the giant's lips and woken him. He opened his eyes and stomped to the entrance of the cave. He saw the men racing down the mountain with their burning leaves.

"That's my fire!" the giant bellowed. He ran down the mountain after the men.

But the men were quick on their feet and reached their cave ahead of the giant. As soon as they got there, they heaved a boulder across the cave's entrance. They then used their flaming leaves to light a wood fire inside the cave.

A few moments later, the giant arrived. He roared and used all his strength to try to move the boulder, but it would not budge. He then had an idea. He would trick the men into moving the boulder, and then he could stick his head into the cave.

"I don't want to hurt you," the giant said in the softest voice he could manage. "I want to be your friend. Move the boulder aside so I can sing to you."

The men did not believe him, but they also did not want to stay in the cave forever, so they heaved the boulder a tiny distance, making a small gap the giant could see through.

"You won't be able to hear me sing through that gap," said the giant. "Push the boulder farther out of the way."

By now, the young men had come up with a plan. "Okay," they called. "We'll move the boulder."

The men shifted the boulder again until the giant could fit his head into the gap. But before he could open his mouth, the men pushed the boulder forward, extinguishing his fire forever.

The men ran from the cave, shouting the news to the village. They shared the flames with all the villagers. From that time on, everyone on the island had a fire burning in their huts to cook their food and keep them warm at night.

THE GIANT WITH TEETH OF FIRE

| **Literal** | Find the answers directly in the text. |

1. What caused the giant to wake up?

_____

_____

2. Order these events from 1 to 5.

  a. _____ The giant chased the men down the mountain.

  b. _____ The men gathered dried leaves.

  c. _____ The giant's teeth were extinguished.

  d. _____ The giant said he wanted to sing to the men.

  e. _____ The men lit a wood fire.

| **Inferential** | Think about what the text says. |

1. Why do you think the giant used a soft voice to talk to the men?

_____

_____

_____

2. Write points for or against this statement: "The men in the folktale were clever." Do you agree or disagree with this statement? Give reasons to support your claim.

_____

_____

_____

_____

_____

THE GIANT WITH TEETH OF FIRE

Applied   Use what you know about the text and your own experience.

1. Do you think the giant deserved having his fire extinguished?   ☐ Yes   ☐ No

Write reasons for your answer.

_____

_____

_____

_____

_____

_____

2. Write a different ending for this folktale.

_____

_____

_____

_____

_____

_____

_____

_____

_____

_____

_____

_____

THE GIANT WITH TEETH OF FIRE

Use the text on page 55 to help you complete this activity. Congratulations! You have been chosen to direct the movie version of "The Giant with Teeth of Fire." The scriptwriters want you to make the movie a thrilling experience for the audience. You begin by planning the most exciting scenes.

1. Describe two parts of the story you think will make exciting scenes.

- _____
  _____
  _____
- _____
  _____
  _____

2. Imagine the two parts you have chosen as movie scenes. Write what you think the audience should see and hear for each scene. For example, "The scene begins with a close-up of the giant's feet thundering on the ground. The camera moves to the villagers' horrified faces and we hear their screams over mournful music."

Scene 1	Scene 2
Title: _____	Title: _____
Sights and sounds:	Sights and sounds:
_____	_____
_____	_____
_____	_____
_____	_____
_____	_____
_____	_____
_____	_____
_____	_____
_____	_____

Genre: Suspense

READING FOCUS

- Analyzes and extracts information from a suspense narrative to answer literal, inferential, and applied questions
- Uses sensory imaging to create appropriate background information for a suspense story
- Predicts likely events that could take place after the close of a suspense story

ANSWER KEY

Literal (Page 61)

1. 12 years old
2. His mother had called him for dinner.
3. the bed, in front of the door, in front of Ryan's face

Inferential (Page 61)

1. Three of the following: starts to shiver or shudder; tries to scream for his parents; feels sweat prickling the back of his neck; staggers backward and falls to his knees; whimpers to the clown
2. The author may want the reader to use his or her imagination.
3. Answers/drawings will vary.

Applied (Page 62)

1–2. Answers/drawings will vary.

Applying Strategies (Page 63)

1–2. Answers will vary.

EXTENSIONS

- Other suspense stories students may enjoy include the following:
  - *The Graveyard Book* by Neil Gaiman
  - *His Dark Materials Omnibus* by Philip Pullman
  - *The Invention of Hugo Cabaret* by Brian Selznick

STOP CLOWNING AROUND!

Name _____

Read the suspense narrative and answer the questions on the following pages.

Ryan put the clown on his bookcase and made a face at it. He couldn't believe that his Aunt Jane would give him a present like that for his 12th birthday. It was a toy meant for a little kid! She'd always given him such great presents up until now. And then this had arrived in the mail yesterday. Without even a card.

"Ryan! Time for dinner!"

"Coming, Mom." Ryan gave the clown one more disgusted glance and then raced down the stairs.

After dinner, he went up to his room to grab a book to read. His father was watching a boring show on television, and he didn't feel like playing on the computer.

As Ryan walked into the room, he suddenly started to shiver. *Someone is watching me.* The thought went through his mind before he could stop it. What had made him think that? He'd probably been watching too many scary movies lately. But then he looked at his bookcase. The clown was missing. Ryan gasped and then laughed at himself when he saw it sitting on his bed. He must have put it there without realizing. He shook his head and left the room. But it was strange. He was sure that it had been on the bookcase . . .

A few hours later it was bedtime. Ryan had almost forgotten about the clown until he walked into his room again. The same cold shudder went through him, and his eyes went straight to his bed. The clown wasn't there.

Bang! Ryan's door slammed shut behind him. He whirled around. The clown was sitting in front of the door, its glassy eyes boring into Ryan's. Ryan tried to scream out for his parents, but the words got stuck in his throat. He reached out for the door handle, but some invisible force pushed him back. Ryan felt the sweat start to prickle the back of his neck. He looked down at the clown. Its face had contorted into an ominous expression. And then it started to rise, slowly and gently in the air, until it was directly in front of Ryan's terrified face.

Ryan tried to scream again, but his voice simply wouldn't work. He staggered backward and fell to his knees.

"Please," he whimpered. "Don't hurt me. What do you want? Why did Aunt Jane send you?"

STOP CLOWNING AROUND!

Literal   Find the answers directly in the text.

1. How old is Ryan? _____

2. Why did Ryan go downstairs?

   _____

   _____

3. List the three places the clown moves to.

   • _____   • _____

   • _____

Inferential   Think about what the text says.

1. List three things Ryan does that tell us he is uneasy or frightened.

   • _____

   • _____

   • _____

2. Why do you think the author intentionally left out a description of the clown?

   _____

   _____

3. Describe and draw the clown as you imagined it.

   _____

   _____

   _____

   _____

STOP CLOWNING AROUND!

Applied   Use what you know about the text and your own experience.

1. The author presents the clown as a frightening object by making it come to life and do unexpected things. Choose a toy from the list below. Write a description of the toy, and explain what makes it seem frightening.

☐ doll   ☐ toy truck   ☐ building blocks   ☐ jumprope   ☐ other: _____

_____

_____

_____

_____

_____

_____

_____

2. Draw a picture of the toy from question #1, and try to depict what makes it seem frightening.

STOP CLOWNING AROUND!

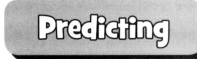

Suspense stories like the one on page 60 are designed to frighten a reader. They often contain supernatural events, such as ghosts, aliens, or objects that come to life. The main character is usually in fear. Think carefully about the elements of a typical suspense story to answer the following questions.

1. Invent a backstory for the text on page 60. The backstory is the important background information about the characters or events in the text.

Aunt Jane	The Clown
Is Aunt Jane who Ryan thinks she is? Has something happened to her recently? Did she send the clown to Ryan or did someone else?	How has the clown come to life? Did someone or something help it do this? Why does the clown want to frighten Ryan? What is its goal?
_____	_____
_____	_____
_____	_____
_____	_____
_____	_____
_____	_____
_____	_____
_____	_____

2. Predict what might happen next to Ryan. Write two possibilities.

- _____
  _____
  _____

- _____
  _____
  _____

Genre: Procedure

READING FOCUS

- Analyzes and extracts information from a set of instructions to answer literal, inferential, and applied questions
- Determines the importance of information in a text to create a cartoon strip with dialogue
- Uses sensory imaging to visualize himself/herself performing a magic trick

ANSWER KEY

Literal (Page 66)

1. On the table, under the napkin.

2. a. True   b. True   c. False   d. False

Inferential (Page 66)

1. Answer(s) will vary. Possible answer(s): the saltshaker could fall from your lap, the napkin could tear, the napkin may not hold the shape of the saltshaker.

2. a. The napkin has to be thick so that it can hold the shape of the saltshaker.

   b. The audience is told that the coin will disappear so that their eyes will be focused on the coin and not the saltshaker.

3. The magician has to secretly pick up the saltshaker from his or her lap so that the audience doesn't figure out that the saltshaker was dropped into the magician's lap.

Applied (Page 67)

1. Answers will vary. Possible answer(s): good entertainer, creative, charismatic, sleight of hand.

2. Answers will vary.

Applying Strategies (Page 68)

Answers/drawings will vary.

EXTENSIONS

- Some suitable titles about magic tricks or practical jokes for children include the following:
  - *The Practical Joker's Handbook* by John Dineen
  - *Magic Tricks* by Fay Presto
  - *Amazing Magic Tricks* by Thomas Canavan

THE SALTSHAKER TRICK

Name _____

Read the magic trick instructions and answer the questions on the following pages.

The Trick:

You announce to your audience that you are going to use a saltshaker to push a coin through a table. You cover the saltshaker with a napkin and say some magic words . . . what happened? It's not the coin that has gone through the table—it's the saltshaker!

You Will Need:

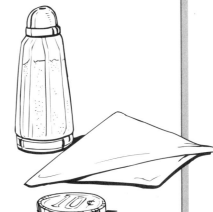

- a saltshaker with a pointed top
- a coin
- a thick paper napkin

What To Do:

1. Sit at a table and place the coin in front of you.

2. Put the saltshaker on top of the coin and cover it with the napkin. Place both of your hands firmly around the saltshaker to make sure the napkin takes on the shape of the saltshaker.

3. Pick up the saltshaker, covered by the napkin, and demonstrate the coin is still on the table. Meanwhile, move the saltshaker over the edge of the table until it is above your lap.

4. Secretly drop the saltshaker into your lap. The napkin will keep its shape, making it look as if you are still holding the saltshaker.

5. Place the napkin back over the coin. Then quickly bang your fist on the napkin. Pretend to be amazed as the napkin flattens onto the table—the saltshaker has disappeared!

6. Reach under the table and secretly pick up the saltshaker from your lap. Then take a bow!

THE SALTSHAKER TRICK

Literal   Find the answers directly in the text.

1. Where is the coin at the end of the trick? _____

2. Read each sentence. Decide if each statement is **True** or **False**.

   a. You need to sit at a table to perform this trick.   ☐ True ☐ False

   b. When you begin the trick, the audience thinks that   ☐ True ☐ False
      you want to make the coin go through the table.

   c. You could do this trick without covering the saltshaker.   ☐ True ☐ False

   d. It is okay if the audience sees you pick up the saltshaker   ☐ True ☐ False
      from your lap.

Inferential   Think about what the text says.

1. List some things that could go wrong with this trick.

   _____

   _____

2. Why do you think:

   a. the napkin has to be thick? _____

   _____

   b. the audience is told that the coin, not the saltshaker, will disappear? _____

   _____

3. Why does the magician have to secretly pick up the saltshaker from his or her lap?

   _____

   _____

THE SALTSHAKER TRICK

Applied   Use what you know about the text and your own experience.

1. What do you think makes a good magician? List three qualities you think the ideal magician should have.

   - _____

   - _____

   - _____

2. Write a procedure for a magic trick you know.

   The Trick:

   _____

   _____

   _____

   _____

   You Will Need:

   _____

   _____

   _____

   What to Do:

   _____

   _____

   _____

   _____

   _____

   _____

   _____

THE SALTSHAKER TRICK

Use the text on page 65 to help you complete this activity. Magicians usually talk a lot while they are performing. They do this to engage the audience as to what is happening or perceive to be happening.

Imagine yourself performing the trick described on page 65. Create a cartoon strip showing the six steps. Write what you would say during each step of the trick. It should sound impressive to an audience.

1

_____
_____
_____
_____

2

_____
_____
_____

3

_____
_____
_____

4

_____
_____
_____
_____

5

_____
_____
_____
_____

6

_____
_____
_____
_____

68

Teacher Information

READING FOCUS

- Analyzes and extracts information from a play to answer literal, inferential, and applied questions
- Determines the important elements of a play to write a plan
- Summarizes a newly created version of a play

ANSWER KEY

Literal (Page 71)

1. She had broken a mirror and bought some shoes.
2. a. 4   b. 3   c. 2   d. 5   e. 1
3. The quiche Flynn was making for lunch.

Inferential (Page 71)

1. Natalie has just shown that she is superstitious, too.
2. She cannot believe that Flynn is still superstitious.

Applied (Page 72)

1–2. Answers will vary.

Applying Strategies (Page 73)

1–2. Answers will vary.

EXTENSIONS

- The class can read and perform plays adapted from popular children's books, such as the following:
  - *Charlie and the Chocolate Factory* by Roald Dahl
  - *Charlotte's Web* by E.B. White
  - *Hating Alison Ashley* by Robin Klein
  - *The Lion, the Witch and the Wardrobe* by C.S. Lewis

SUPERSTITIOUS

Name _____

Read the play and answer the questions on the following pages.

Flynn is in his house, setting the table for lunch. He hears a knock at the door and walks over to open it. His friend Natalie is standing there, carrying an umbrella and a shopping bag.

Natalie   Hi, Flynn! Thanks for inviting me for lunch. *(She points offstage.)* Is that your black cat? I almost tripped over it.

Flynn   No, that's the neighbor's cat. Don't tell me it crossed your path? That's very bad luck.

Natalie   *(sighing)* You're not still superstitious, are you?

Flynn   Well, maybe a bit. I just think it's best to avoid things that might be bad luck. Anyway, come in. It's great to see you.

Natalie   *(stepping inside)* Do you mind if I leave my umbrella here to dry? *(She opens it and props it against the wall.)*

Flynn   Natalie! Didn't I ever tell you it's bad luck to open an umbrella indoors?

Natalie   *(laughing)* I don't believe in things like that.

Flynn and Natalie walk into Flynn's kitchen.

Natalie   (sniffing the air) Mmm, what's that delicious smell?

Flynn   I've made a quiche. I know it's your favorite. Please sit down. It's nearly ready. *(Flynn gestures toward the kitchen table.)*

Natalie   Thanks. *(She sits down and puts her shopping bag on the table.)*

Flynn   *(sitting next to her)* What's in the bag?

Natalie   Just a pair of shoes I bought on the way here. They were on sale and . . .

Flynn   Oh, no. Take them off the table. Now!

Natalie   Why . . . oh, that's right. Shoes on the table are supposed to bring bad luck, aren't they? Okay, I'll take them off if it will make you feel better. *(She picks up the bag and puts it on the floor.)* I'd better not tell you about the mirror I broke this morning—that brings me bad luck too, doesn't it?

Flynn   *(groaning)* Yes—for the next seven years! *(He shakes his head.)* Let's change the subject. When do you go on your vacation?

Natalie   Tomorrow.

Flynn   But that's Friday the thirteenth! You can't go then!

Natalie   Flynn, I already told you I don't believe in all that nonsense about bad luck. And anyway *(reaching into her pocket)*, I don't go anywhere without my four-leaf clover lucky charm. *(She knocks on the wooden table.)* I'll be just fine.

Natalie looks puzzled as Flynn bursts out laughing.

SUPERSTITIOUS

1. Write two things Natalie had done before arriving at Flynn's house.

_____

_____

2. Order these events from 1–5.

    a. _____ Natalie takes the shoes off the table.

    b. _____ Flynn sits at the table.

    c. _____ Flynn and Natalie walk into the kitchen.

    d. _____ Natalie knocks on the table.

    e. _____ Natalie opens her umbrella.

3. What could Natalie smell?

_____

_____

1. Why does Flynn laugh at the end of the play?

_____

_____

2. Why do you think Natalie sighs near the beginning of the play?

_____

_____

_____

SUPERSTITIOUS

Applied   Use what you know about the text and your own experience.

1. Place an **X** on the scale to show how superstitious you are.

not at all   extremely

If you are superstitious, explain what you are superstitious about. If you are not superstitious, explain why.

_____
_____
_____
_____
_____
_____

2. List some good and bad luck superstitions not mentioned in the play.

Good Luck	**Bad Luck**

Name _____

SUPERSTITIOUS

Determining Importance

The plans of stories and plays are constructed by authors in many different ways. The author of the play on page 70 used the following steps:

- Decided on a suitable setting and characters for a short play about superstitions.
- Made a list of common bad and good luck superstitions.
- Thought of a series of events that would cause the characters to experience or discuss each bad luck superstition.
- Used the good-luck superstitions to create a humorous ending.

1. Imagine you are the author of "Superstitious." Write a plan for your own version of the play by following the steps above.

Setting	
Characters	**Relationship of Characters** (e.g., "friends," "husband/wife," etc.)

Bad-Luck Superstitions

- _____
- _____
- _____

Good-Luck Superstitions

- _____   • _____

Series of Events

- _____
- _____
- _____

Ending

2. Use your answers to question #1 to help you write your own play about superstitions. You can use some of the ideas from the original play. Write your play on a separate sheet of paper, and then use it to write your playscript.

Genre: Letter to the Editor

READING FOCUS

- Analyzes and extracts information from a letter to the editor to answer literal, inferential, and applied questions

- Scans a text for information to answer interview questions

- Compares the decisions of a fictional character with those he or she might make about an issue

ANSWER KEY

Literal (Page 76)

1. The snacks it sells are overpriced, and it stocks a limited range of refreshments.

2. a. False   b. False   c. True   d. True

Inferential (Page 76)

1. The writer calls the owners greedy because they have no problem overcharging people for food sold at their concession stand.

2. Answers will vary.

Applied (Page 77)

1. Answers will vary. Possible answer(s):

   For—support the residents of Hamilton, save money by going to the movies in Newbury, it may urge the owners to change this rule

   Against—drive farther to Newbury, not supporting local businesses

2. Answers will vary.

Applying Strategies (Page 78)

1–5. Answers will vary.

EXTENSIONS

- Students can collect some interesting letters to the editor from local newspapers and discuss the issues contained in them.

- Students can choose an article from a newspaper and write a letter to the editor, stating their opinion about the piece.

CINEMA SITUATION

Name _____

Read the letter to the editor and answer the questions on the following pages.

15 Wexford Place
Hamilton, Alabama

May 11, 2014

The Editor
Western Ridge News
21 Knight Road
Hamilton, Alabama

Dear Madam,

Your report about the Hamilton movie theater complex's decision to ban movie-goers from bringing their own food and drinks into movie theaters had my blood boiling! I am shocked and amazed that the ban even includes homemade snacks.

Not surprisingly, the movie theater complex owners are perfectly happy with people buying food at the theater's concession stand. But the snacks offered for sale can be bought at any supermarket for less than half the price! The concession stand also stocks a limited range of refreshments. What if some movie-goers are allergic to the products sold at the concession stand? Does this mean they have to go hungry or thirsty?

I am also wondering how the theater owners intend to police the ban. Should we expect bag checks by snack-sniffing dogs before we are allowed in? Will "illegal" snacks be confiscated?

The whole idea is simply ridiculous. All that it will achieve for the theater owners is having to turn their customers away. Since hearing of the ban, many of my friends and I now prefer to drive an extra 10 minutes to go to the movies in Newbury rather than give any money to these greedy people.

I am asking for all residents of Hamilton to boycott the movie theater complex completely until its owners change this rule. We need to stand together on this issue. No one should have the right to tell us what we can and can't eat!

Yours sincerely,

Clare Warden

CINEMA SITUATION

Literal   Find the answers directly in the text.

1. What does the writer dislike about the movie theater concession stand?

_____

_____

_____

2. Read each sentence. Decide if each statement is **True** or **False**.

a. The cinema complex owners are using snack-sniffing dogs.   ☐ True ☐ False

b. You could take a homemade cake into the Hamilton movie theater.   ☐ True ☐ False

c. There is a movie theater in Newbury.   ☐ True ☐ False

d. The editor of the *Western Ridge News* is a woman.   ☐ True ☐ False

Inferential   Think about what the text says.

1. Why do you think the writer calls the Hamilton movie theater complex owners "greedy people"?

_____

_____

_____

2. Do you think the Hamilton movie theater complex owners have made a wise decision? Give reasons for your answer.

_____

_____

_____

_____

_____

CINEMA SITUATION

Use what you know about the text and your own experience.

1. Imagine you are trying to decide whether or not to join the writer's boycott of the movie theater. Write a list of reasons for and against the boycott.

For	Against

2. Write a letter to the editor from an owner of the Hamilton movie theater justifying your decision.

Dear Madam, _____

_____

_____

_____

_____

_____

_____

_____

_____

_____

_____

_____

CINEMA SITUATION

Use the text on page 75 to help you complete this activity. Find a partner to work with. Imagine you are the owners of the Hamilton movie theater complex. A journalist from the *Western Ridge News* comes to see you to ask you questions about your food and drink ban. He explains that the answers will be published in an article in the next issue of the newspaper. Write your answers to the journalist's questions.

1. Why did you decide to ban people from bringing their own food and drink into your movie theaters? Do you think this is fair?

_____

_____

_____

2. Do you think you should improve what your concession stand has to offer? Why/Why not?

_____

_____

_____

3. People might try to smuggle "banned" food and drinks into your movie theaters. How will you control this?

_____

_____

_____

4. What is your opinion of the letter to the editor written by Clare Warden, which was published recently in our newspaper?

_____

_____

_____

5. Will you change your minds about your decision? Why/Why not?

_____

_____

_____

Genre: Biography

READING FOCUS

- Analyzes and extracts information from a biography to answer literal, inferential, and applied questions
- Scans a biography for facts to complete a timeline
- Scans a biography for facts about a person's achievements
- Makes connections between an individual from a biography and himself or herself

ANSWER KEY

Literal (Page 81)

1. He traveled and worked around Italy.
2. *The Baptism of Christ, The Last Supper,* and the *Mona Lisa.*

Inferential (Page 81)

1. a. Opinion   b. Opinion   c. Fact   d. Opinion
2. Answers will vary. Possible answer(s): Da Vinci was skilled in so many areas, he conceptualized many modern inventions years before they were even invented, he was the first scientist to study the flight of birds, he drew the first correct representation of human body parts.
3. Answers will vary.

Applied (Page 82)

1–3. Answers will vary.

Applying Strategies (Page 83)

1.

1452	born near the town of Vinci in Italy
1473	as an apprentice for del Verrocchio, da Vinci painted part of *The Baptism of Christ*
1482	da Vinci became the court artist and engineer for the Duke of Milan
1499	da Vinci fled from Milan when it was attacked by French troops
1516	da Vinci was invited to France to become the official painter, engineer, and architect for King Francis I

Art: *The Baptism of Christ, The Last Supper, Mona Lisa*
Science: first scientist to study the flight of birds, drew the first correct representation of human body parts
Inventive Ideas: drew plans for a type of helicopter, an airplane, military weapons, parachutes, and submarines; imagined water inventions, such as underwater breathing devices, life preservers, shoes to help you walk on water, and swimming fins; designed a bike hundreds of years before it was invented

2–3. Answers will vary.

EXTENSIONS

- Further information about Leonardo da Vinci can be found by entering his name into a search engine. Some useful websites include the following:
  - *http://legacy.mos.org/sln/leonardo/*
  - *http://www.lairweb.org.nz/leonardo/*
- Students can search the Internet to find out about the life of a person that interests them and use it to write a profile about him or her.

Name _____

Read the biography and answer the questions on the following pages.

Leonardo da Vinci is regarded as one of the greatest geniuses of all time. He was a skilled artist, inventor, architect, and scientist—among other things!

Da Vinci was born in 1452 near the town of Vinci in Italy. As a teenager, he became an apprentice to a well-known artist, Andrea del Verrocchio, in the city of Florence. During this time, da Vinci learned painting, sculpting, and other crafts. When da Vinci was about 21, del Verrocchio let him paint part of an important painting, *The Baptism of Christ.*

In 1482, da Vinci became the court artist and engineer for the Duke of Milan. During his 17 years in Milan, da Vinci designed forts, weapons, sets for plays, and canal systems. He also wrote his ideas on a vast range of subjects, from human anatomy to flying machines. Amazingly, he even found time to work on many paintings, although he left dozens of these unfinished. One that he did manage to complete was the famous wall mural *The Last Supper.*

In 1499, da Vinci had to flee Milan when it was attacked by French troops. He then spent several years traveling and working around Italy. In 1516, he was invited to France to become the official painter, engineer, and architect for King Francis I. Here he completed plans for buildings, as well as sketches of animals, machines, and studies on the nature of water.

Da Vinci died in France in 1519. He had recorded his ideas, observations, plans, and sketches in a series of notebooks throughout his life, but unfortunately, these were not found until hundreds of years after his death. In the meantime, other people came up with the same or similar ideas. You may be surprised to learn that some modern inventions were once drawn or described by da Vinci.

Just a few examples of da Vinci's achievements include the following:

- He drew plans for a type of helicopter, an airplane, military weapons, parachutes, and submarines.

- He was the first scientist to study the flight of birds.

- He drew the first correct representation of human body parts, which included bones, muscles, and organs. He got his information from studying human corpses.

- He painted the *Mona Lisa,* one of the most famous paintings in the world.

- He was very interested in water and imagined inventions like underwater breathing devices, life preservers, shoes to help you walk on water, and swimming fins.

Think about Leonardo da Vinci the next time you ride a bike. He even came up with a design for that—hundreds of years before it was actually invented!

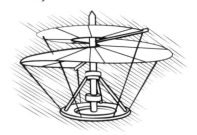

LEONARDO DA VINCI

Literal   Find the answers directly in the text.

1. What did da Vinci do between 1499 and 1516?

_____

_____

2. List the titles of three paintings da Vinci worked on.

- _____

- _____

- _____

Inferential   Think about what the text says.

1. Read each sentence. For each statement, decide whether each sentence is a **Fact** or an **Opinion**.

a. Da Vinci should have published his ideas in books.　☐ Fact ☐ Opinion

b. Da Vinci is the smartest person ever to have lived.　☐ Fact ☐ Opinion

c. Most of da Vinci's life was spent in Italy.　☐ Fact ☐ Opinion

d. Da Vinci should have concentrated on one occupation.　☐ Fact ☐ Opinion

2. Why do you think da Vinci is regarded as a genius?

_____

_____

3. What do you think was da Vinci's greatest achievement? Explain why.

_____

_____

_____

_____

LEONARDO DA VINCI

Applied   Use what you know about the text and your own experience.

1. One of da Vinci's ideas for an invention was shoes that could help you walk on water. Why might these be useful for a person or a company to own? List some ideas below.

_____

_____

_____

_____

_____

2. Leonardo was a skilled artist, inventor, architect, and scientist. Think about your skills and what you are interested in. Write about your skills and what you would like to possibly do with your skills in the future.

_____

_____

_____

_____

_____

3. What is your favorite invention that you use? Who invented it, and what year was it invented?

Invention: _____

Inventor: _____

Year Invented: _____

Why is this invention so important to you?

_____

_____

_____

LEONARDO DA VINCI

Use the text on **page 80** to help you complete this activity. Imagine that Leonardo da Vinci invents a time machine in 1516. He uses it to travel forward in time to the present day. You are lucky enough to be chosen to interview him.

1. Prepare your interview by noting some background information on da Vinci. Complete a timeline of important events in his life and list some of his great achievements.

Timeline

1452
1473
1482
1499
1516

Examples of Achievements

Art: _____

_____

_____

Science: _____

_____

_____

Inventive Ideas: _____

_____

_____

2. Write three questions you would like to ask da Vinci.

- _____
- _____
- _____

3. Imagine meeting da Vinci in the present, and he tells you that he is interested in seeing some modern inventions. List three things you would like to show him. Explain why you think he would be interested in each one.

- _____
- _____
  _____
- _____
  _____

Genre: Journalistic Writing—
Newspaper Report

READING FOCUS

- Analyzes and extracts information from a newspaper article to answer literal, inferential, and applied questions
- Scans a text for different points of view
- Predicts the likely reactions of a fictional person

ANSWER KEY

Literal (Page 86)

1. a. 2 years ago   b. 19th century   c. 24 years old   d. 14

2. art museums in France

3. a. art historian

    b. artist

    c. schoolteacher

    d. artist and historian

Inferential (Page 86)

1. Answers will vary.

2. Answers will vary. Possible answer(s): nostalgic about her grandfather, indifferent, annoyed about trying to figure out what to do with the painting.

Applied (Page 87)

1–2. Answers will vary.

Applying Strategies (Page 88)

1. Miss Sinclair: given to her by her grandfather, he bought it at a flea market in France

Mr. Clifton: the signature matches perfectly, Morel's age is written underneath the signature, Morel did many paintings of cats

Mr. Marceau: the style is completely different, Morel's diaries state that he did not begin painting until he was at least 15, Marceau's research does not show that Morel completed this painting

2. Answers will vary.

EXTENSIONS

- Students can collect articles from newspapers and the Internet. Discuss the type of language used by the majority of the articles.
- Students can rewrite the headlines from articles read in newspapers or on the Internet.

Name _____

Read the newspaper article and answer the questions on the following pages.

Garden Shed Find "Worth Millions," Says Expert

A young schoolteacher has found a painting in her garden shed that has caused great excitement among art historians—and could be worth millions.

Genevieve Sinclair, 24, was cleaning out the shed when she discovered an oil painting of a cat sitting in front of a fireplace.

"The painting was given to me by my grandfather just before he died, two years ago," said Miss Sinclair. "He bought it at a flea market in France. I had completely forgotten it was in the shed. Although Grandad always told me it was valuable, I didn't really believe him. I had always disliked the painting and thought I would eventually sell it in a garage sale."

That was until an artist friend of Miss Sinclair's saw the painting and spotted the signature scrawled in the bottom corner— "Claude Morel." He urged Miss Sinclair to take the painting to a local university. And it was there, in the company of art historian Eric Clifton, that Miss Sinclair discovered the painting's true worth.

"Most people will know Claude Morel's name—he was an important French artist of the 19th century," said Mr. Clifton. "It was thought that all of his works were held in various art museums in France. But this painting was unknown. It is definitely his. The signature matches perfectly, and he has written his age—14—underneath the painting, as he did with all of his works. He also did many paintings of cats. This find could be worth millions for Miss Sinclair."

Other art experts, however, don't share Mr. Clifton's enthusiasm. Many are suggesting that the painting is a fake.

"I have examined the painting, and I don't believe it was painted by Morel," says renowned French artist and historian, Guy Marceau. "The style is completely different from all of his other paintings. Also, Claude Morel's diaries tell us that he did not begin painting until he was at least 15. I have written three books on the life of Morel, and I can assure you they are 100-percent correct in every detail. None of my research shows that he completed this painting."

It appears that Miss Sinclair will have to wait at least six months before experts can tell her whether or not the painting is genuine. In the meantime, she admits she is dreaming about all the money she might make.

"It would completely change my life," she said. "I can't wait to find out whether or not I am a millionaire."

THE PAINTING IN THE SHED

Literal   Find the answers directly in the text.

1. Answer the following questions.

    a. How many years ago did Miss Sinclair's grandfather die?   _____

    b. In which century did Morel complete his paintings?   _____

    c. How old is Miss Sinclair?   _____

    d. What is written under Morel's signature on the painting found in Miss Sinclair's shed?   _____

2. Where could you go to see a collection of Morel's paintings?

    _____

3. List the occupations of each of these people.

    a. Eric Clifton   b. Claude Morel

    _____   _____

    c. Genevieve Sinclair   d. Guy Marceau

    _____   _____

Inferential   Think about what the text says.

1. Write an alternative, eye-catching headline for this article.

    _____

2. List three emotions Miss Sinclair might have felt when she first saw the painting in her shed.

    • _____

    • _____

    • _____

THE PAINTING IN THE SHED

Applied   Use what you know about the text and your own experience.

1. Imagine you are Miss Sinclair and you have been told the painting is genuine. You will soon be a millionaire! What will you do with the money?

_____

_____

_____

_____

_____

_____

_____

_____

_____

2. Another article was written after the painting was declared genuine. Write some statements that may have been quoted from Miss Sinclair.

_____

_____

_____

_____

_____

_____

_____

_____

_____

_____

_____

THE PAINTING IN THE SHED

Use the text on page 85 to complete the activity. Do you think the painting will turn out to be genuine or fake?

1. Write a summary of the evidence given by Miss Sinclair and the two experts to help you make up your mind. Then write your opinion.

Evidence

Miss Sinclair: _____

_____

Mr. Clifton: _____

_____

Mr. Marceau: _____

_____

Based on the evidence, I think the painting is ☐ genuine ☐ a fake

because . . . _____

_____

2. Write what you think each person mentioned in the article would say or do in reaction to each announcement in the newspapers.

Predicting

"Morel painting is genuine"	"Morel painting is a fake"
Miss Sinclair	Miss Sinclair
Mr. Clifton	Mr. Clifton
Mr. Marceau	Mr. Marceau

Genre: Journalistic Writing—Newspaper Report

READING FOCUS

- Analyzes and extracts information from a newspaper article to answer literal, inferential, and applied questions
- Synthesizes information from a text to piece clues together
- Writes a summary to conclude a report

ANSWER KEY

Literal (Page 91)

1. a. 5   b. 6   c. 2   d. 3   e. 1   f. 4
2. a. False   b. True   c. False   d. False   e. True

Inferential (Page 91)

1. Answers will vary. Possible answer(s): panicked, scared, concerned, worried, shocked, stunned, alarmed.
2. Answers will vary.
3. Answers will vary.

Applied (Page 92)

Answers will vary.

Applying Strategies (Page 93)

Answers will vary.

EXTENSIONS

- Students can read articles from newspapers or the Internet and choose one that appeals to them. The students highlight the keywords and phrases of the article and write a summarizing paragraph that records the main idea of the article.
- Students can look at various newspapers and discuss the different sections and topics within the newspaper. The class can then categorize to see what group of people would be interested in which section.

Name _____

Read the newspaper report and answer the questions on the following pages.

Woodvale Morning Herald   *July 17*

BLAZE DESTROYS SCHOOL!

Fourth school in area in past 11 years destroyed by fire during summer vacation

Sirens were heard at Woodvale Middle School yesterday afternoon, but it wasn't the school siren declaring the end of a school day—it was the shrill sound of fire sirens.

The school, which has been closed for the last five weeks for the summer break, was a mass of flames, smoke, and ash yesterday afternoon. The Woodvale Fire Department was contacted at 2:30 p.m. after a local resident, Mrs. Valerie Draper, heard a loud bang . . . "almost like a firework exploding" and noticed smoke coming from the school.

The fire crew arrived to find the science laboratory and neighboring classrooms blazing. The crew was successful in preventing the fire from spreading to the rest of the school.

The principal of Woodvale Middle School, Pat Staines, arrived moments after the fire was extinguished. Mrs. Staines was concerned about the whereabouts of groundskeeper Jim Blackwood, as he was hired to be at the school until 4:00 p.m. each day.

Mr. Blackwood was contacted and found to be at home. He told police that, due to the extremely hot weather, he had left the school at 2:00 p.m. that day.

Mrs. Staines commented that, before the school year ended, the science teacher, Miss Megan Warner, had noticed mouse droppings in the chemical storeroom—a small room attached to the science laboratory. She had informed the principal of her findings, concerned that mice running around in the storeroom could knock chemicals from their shelves. Those chemicals could possibly mix together on the floor of the storeroom—with the potential to cause an explosion, and ultimately, a fire.

Mrs. Staines had asked Mr. Blackwood to take care of the mice situation in the chemical storeroom over the summer break. We have been unsuccessful in our attempts to get Mr. Blackwood to confirm whether he had removed the mice from the storeroom or not.

Woodvale Middle School is the fourth school in the local area to have been damaged by fire during the six-week summer break. Although one school had been the victim of an arson fire, the other two fires had begun in the science laboratories.

BLAZE DESTROYS SCHOOL

Literal   Find the answers directly in the text.

1. Put the chain of events in order from 1–6, with 1 happening first and 6 happening last.

   a. _____ The principal, Pat Staines, arrives at the school.

   b. _____ Journalist asks Jim Blackwood about mice.

   c. _____ Valerie Draper calls emergency services to report a fire.

   d. _____ Fire-engine sirens are heard in the town of Woodvale.

   e. _____ Jim Blackwood leaves the school and goes home.

   f. _____ Firefighters extinguish the fire.

2. Read each sentence. Decide if each statement is **True** or **False**.

   a. Pat Staines called the fire department to report the fire.   ☐ True ☐ False

   b. Megan Warner is the science teacher at Woodvale Middle School.   ☐ True ☐ False

   c. Jim Blackwood left the school early because of the fire.   ☐ True ☐ False

   d. In the past, two schools in the area have been damaged by arsonists.   ☐ True ☐ False

   e. The students at Woodvale are scheduled to return to school in one week.   ☐ True ☐ False

Inferential   Think about what the text says.

1. List some words and phrases to describe how you think the principal felt when she saw the fire engines in front of her school.

   _____

   _____

2. Do you think the noise that Mrs. Draper heard could help explain the cause of the fire? Explain your answer.

   _____

   _____

3. Do you think Jim Blackwood is avoiding answering the journalist? Why do you think this is?

   _____

   _____

BLAZE DESTROYS SCHOOL

Applied   Use what you know about the text and your own experience.

Write an article about the school that was set on fire by an arsonist. Did they catch the arsonist? If so, what clues led the police to the suspect? Make sure to come up with an attention grabbing headline.

Woodvale Morning Herald   *July 20*

_____   _____

_____   _____

_____   _____

_____   _____

_____   _____

_____   _____

_____   _____

_____   _____

_____   _____

_____   _____

_____   _____

_____   _____

_____   _____

_____   _____

_____   _____

_____   _____

Name _____

Applying Strategies

BLAZE DESTROYS SCHOOL

Use the text on page 90 to complete the activity. You are a police officer at the Woodvale Police Department and have been assigned the task of writing the report about the fire at the school. There are three parts to the report.

- You must interview and collect a comment from each person involved.
- You must report on four pieces of evidence that may help to show the cause of the fire.
- You must write a final summary regarding the cause of the fire.

Police Report

Scene: _____

Officer's Name: _____ **Date:** _____

Person Involved	Comment About Cause of Fire
Principal Pat Staines	
Science teacher Megan Warner	
Groundskeeper Jim Blackwood	
Fire chief	

Evidence

Evidence 1	Evidence 2
Evidence 3	Evidence 4

Findings:

_____

_____

Unit 18
The First Spider

Genre: Myth

READING FOCUS

- Analyzes and extracts information from a myth to answer literal, inferential, and applied questions
- Uses synthesis to consider different points of view on the events in a text
- Summarizes the events of a text from a character's point of view
- Makes connections between the events of a text and his or her own opinions

ANSWER KEY

Literal (Page 96)

1. a. True   b. False   c. False   d. True

2. Arachne was too proud and made fun of the gods.

Inferential (Page 96)

1. to see if Arachne really thought she was better than Athena

2. Both tapestries were beautiful and both showed the gods. Athena's tapestry showed the gods performing heroic deeds, and Arachne's tapestry showed the gods in a less favorable light.

3. to punish her for being so boastful and for ridiculing the gods; so people will never again admire her weaving

Applied (Page 97)

1–3. Answers will vary.

Applying Strategies (Page 98)

1–3. Answers will vary.

EXTENSIONS

- More Greek myths can be found in the following books:
  - *Favorite Greek Myths* by Lilian Stoughton Hyde
  - *Greek Myths and Legends* by Anthony Masters
  - *The Orchard Book of Greek Myths* by Geraldine McCaughrean
- Students can read myths from different cultures and compare the common themes.

THE FIRST SPIDER

Name _____

Read the myth and answer the questions on the following pages.

There once was a woman named Arachne who wove beautiful tapestries on her loom. She was so skilled that people came from far away to watch her use her weaving shuttle and thread. They paid great sums of money for her work.

Arachne was very proud of her weaving and boasted about her skills to anyone who would listen.

"I am the best weaver in the world," she said one day. "I am far better than any god or goddess."

An old woman standing nearby heard what she said. "Do you think you are even better than the goddess Athena?" she asked.

Arachne nodded. "Of course," she said, her nose in the air.

Just then, a strong wind whipped up. As it did, the old woman's gray hair became long and golden, and her threadbare coat transformed into a white robe and silver breastplate. Then, the woman grew taller and taller. Arachne blinked. There, towering over her, stood the goddess Athena.

"So you think you weave better tapestries than I do?" asked Athena. "Let us find out. You and I will compete to see who is the best weaver in the world."

Arachne felt a little frightened, but she did not think she could be beaten. She agreed, and the contest began. A crowd gathered to watch.

Athena wove a tapestry that showed the gods performing heroic deeds. They appeared kind, clever, and handsome. The crowd was stunned by the tapestry's beauty.

Arachne wove a tapestry that showed the gods in a less favorable light. They were playing tricks, lazing about, showing off, and arguing. But the crowd could not take its eyes off Arachne's tapestry. It was even more beautiful than Athena's. Arachne had made the scene in her tapestry come to life.

Athena looked carefully at her tapestry and then at Arachne's. "You win," she said. "Your tapestry is better than mine."

Arachne smiled. "I told you so," she said.

The goddess frowned. "But you are too proud, Arachne. And you have made fun of the gods. You must be punished. Never again will people appreciate your work."

With that, the goddess pushed Arachne's shuttle into her mouth. Instantly, Arachne's body began to transform. Her arms became stuck to her sides, leaving her long fingers waving about. Her body became tiny, round, and black. Arachne had become the first spider.

To this day, spiders weave beautiful webs, but they are rarely admired. Most people prefer to knock them down or sweep them away.

THE FIRST SPIDER

Literal   Find the answers directly in the text.

1. Read each sentence. Decide if each statement is **True** or **False**.

    a. Arachne was a boastful person.   ☐ True   ☐ False

    b. Athena wore a golden breastplate.   ☐ True   ☐ False

    c. Arachne's tapestries were cheap to buy.   ☐ True   ☐ False

    d. Arachne's arms became stuck to her sides.   ☐ True   ☐ False

2. Why did Athena frown at Arachne?

_____

_____

Inferential   Think about what the text says.

1. Why do you think Athena disguised herself as an old woman?

_____

_____

2. What did Athena's and Arachne's tapestries have in common? How did they differ?

_____

_____

_____

3. Why do you think the goddess turned Arachne into a spider?

_____

_____

THE FIRST SPIDER

Applied   Use what you know about the text and your own experience.

1. If you were Arachne, would you have agreed to the weaving contest? Explain why/why not.

   _____

   _____

   _____

   _____

2. Write a new ending for the myth after the line, "Never again will people appreciate your work." For example, you might have Athena turn Arachne into a different animal.

   _____

   _____

   _____

   _____

   _____

   _____

   _____

   _____

   _____

3. Imagine that you were in the crowd the day the two competed. Whose tapestry would you have chosen to be the best one? Explain your answer.

   _____

   _____

   _____

   _____

   _____

   _____

THE FIRST SPIDER

Summarizing

Use the text on page 95 to help you complete this activity. Imagine that Zeus, the king of the Greek gods, calls Athena and Arachne before him and asks for an explanation for what happened.

1. Summarize the events in the story from each character's point of view. Include Athena's opinion of Arachne, and Arachne's opinion of Athena.

Athena	Arachne

2. After listening to the evidence, Zeus gives a written judgment on what happened to Arachne. Write what you think it might say.

_____

_____

_____

3. What is your opinion about what happened? Do you think it is fair that Arachne was punished for showing off? Give reasons for your answer.

_____

_____

_____

98

READING FOCUS

- Analyzes and extracts information from an exposition to answer literal, inferential, and applied questions
- Scans an exposition for information
- Paraphrases information from a text to complete an exposition template

ANSWER KEY

Literal (Page 101)

1. a. Fact   b. Fact   c. Opinion   d. Fact   e. Opinion   f. Opinion

2. The writer suggests wrapping oneself in an invisible cloak once a new baby arrives in the family.

3. The toddler is referred to as a "tiny tornado" because he or she slobbers over toys and bulldozes constructions to the ground.

Inferential (Page 101)

1. It means trying to get attention from the parents either through good or bad behavior. Examples will vary.

2. Answers will vary. Possible answer(s): angry, frustrated, irritated, upset, annoyed.

Applied (Page 102)

1–2. Answers will vary.

Applying Strategies (Page 103)

Answers will vary.

EXTENSIONS

- Students can use the template on page 103 to write an exposition from a different point of view. Students can write a final draft and ask a partner to read it, checking that it makes sense and that the criteria for an exposition have been met.
- The teacher can extend the activity further by preparing students for a "mini-debate" that focuses on the pros and cons of being the oldest or youngest, etc.

Name _____

Read the exposition and answer the questions on the following pages.

Being the oldest child in the family is just one big headache!

As the firstborn, you have your mom and dad all to yourself, and everything is perfect! Every little thing you do is new and cute, and hundreds of pictures are taken, capturing your every expression and new trick.

This all changes the minute a new baby arrives. You might as well wrap yourself in an invisible cloak because the only time you are called is when you are needed to "help with the baby" or when you are getting scolded for "attention-seeking behavior"!

As the baby grows, your toys are slobbered over and clever constructions bulldozed to the ground by the tiny tornado known as the "toddler." Parents, who had always been fair and listened to your cries of injustice in the past, now respond to your complaints with sickening comments like, "But he's just a baby!"

Once the younger sibling is old enough to go to school, your whole world changes again. The walk to school, which had once been a great time to catch up with your friends, is now shadowed by a dark cloud known as responsibility! Do you have any idea how stressful it is trying to make a menacing munchkin hold your hand and look "left, right, left" before crossing the street?

Once he or she is at your school, you are never free! You could be playing basketball with your friends at lunchtime—about to make a wicked three-pointer—when younger sibling runs up to you, complaining about a nasty "bigger kid." (Do I look like a bodyguard?) Your friends look at you like it is your duty to go and defend the little terror.

In general, the oldest sibling is given a raw deal! We are disappointed once we realize we are not the center of our parents' universe, our toys and games suffer, and we are burdened with the extra responsibilities that come with being the oldest. Please, moms and dads, show some sympathy for your firstborn—especially when shopping for our next birthday present!

FIRSTBORN FURY!

Literal   Find the answers directly in the text.

1. Decide if each sentence is **Fact** or **Opinion**.

    a. The writer has a younger sibling.   ☐ Fact ☐ Opinion

    b. The younger sibling is a boy.   ☐ Fact ☐ Opinion

    c. The writer has a birthday coming up.   ☐ Fact ☐ Opinion

    d. The writer plays basketball.   ☐ Fact ☐ Opinion

    e. All little brothers and sisters break toys. ☐ Fact ☐ Opinion

    f. It is easier being the youngest child than ☐ Fact ☐ Opinion
       it is being the oldest.

2. What event causes the writer to suggest using an invisible cloak?

    _____

    _____

3. Why does the writer refer to a toddler as a "tiny tornado"?

    _____

    _____

Inferential   Think about what the text says.

1. What do you think the writer means by "attention-seeking behavior"? Give an example.

    _____

    _____

2. Write words and phrases to describe how the writer most likely feels when his toys are slobbered over and broken by his younger brother.

    _____

    _____

Name _____

Activities

FIRSTBORN FURY!

Applied Use what you know about the text and your own experience.

1. **Your friends look at you like it is your duty to go and defend the little terror.**

   Do you think it is an older sibling's "duty" to protect younger brothers and sisters from bullies in school? Explain your answer.

   _____

   _____

   _____

   _____

   _____

   _____

   _____

   _____

   _____

2. Do you think there might be times when the older sibling likes having a younger brother or sister? Give reasons and examples.

   _____

   _____

   _____

   _____

   _____

   _____

   _____

   _____

   _____

#8248 Comprehending Text   102   ©*Teacher Created Resources*

FIRSTBORN FURY!

Use the text on page 100 to help you complete this activity. An exposition is written to persuade others to a particular point of view. Expositions follow a set structure. Find examples in the text for each of the following. Do not copy the sentences exactly—write the main idea.

Exposition

Begin with a strong opening statement that presents the writer's opinion:

_____

_____

Present reasons to support the opinion and give evidence and examples:

Reason 1:	Reason 2:
Reason 3:	**Reason 4:**

Include rhetorical questions to encourage the reader to agree with a point of view. (A rhetorical question is a question for which an answer is not expected.)

_____

_____

The final paragraph—restate the opinion of the writer, and list the main reasons why the reader should agree.

_____

_____

Genre: Science Fiction

READING FOCUS

- Analyzes and extracts information from a science-fiction text to answer literal, inferential, and applied questions
- Paraphrases the main ideas and moral of a story
- Determines the importance of information in a text to create a storyboard strip

ANSWER KEY

Literal (Page 106)

1. a. 3   b. 1   c. 2   d. 5   e. 4

2. Bailey jumped and ran in midair to avoid being struck by sharp, star-shaped objects that were being thrown at him by a monkey.

Inferential (Page 106)

1. No: Bailey had a routine that helped him to deal with the long school day.

2. Bailey was out of shape because he spent most of his time playing video games instead of being active.

3. He used to enjoy spending his time playing video games, but after his experience, he would much rather spend more time playing outside.

Applied (Page 107)

1. Answers will vary. Possible answer(s): doesn't like video games, thinks that video games are unhealthy.

2. Answers will vary.

3. Answers will vary. Possible answer(s): spend more time with family, healthier, be in better shape, more time for reading.

Applying Strategies (Page 108)

1. Answers should indicate that Bailey somehow was transported into a video game where he faced danger. He then promised himself that if he were to get out of the situation, he would play less video games and play more outside. He was quickly brought back into his living room, where his life changed for the better. Since that day, Bailey chooses to lead a more active lifestyle.

2. Answers and drawings will vary.

EXTENSIONS

- Collate data from the class about how the students spend their free time. Create a class graph of the information. Compare the results of time spent playing computer games (or in front of a television screen) to time spent being active. Hold discussions with the class regarding the results. In groups, students can create an action plan to increase the time all children spend being active.

- Students may enjoy reading other science-fiction stories, such as the following:
  - *The Golden Compass* by Philip Pullman
  - *The Angel Factory* by Terence Blacker
  - *The Exchange Student* by Kate Gilmore
  - *Earthborn* by Sylvia Waugh
  - *Space Race* by Sylvia Waugh

CHANGE YOUR LIFE!

Name _____

Read the science-fiction story and answer the questions on the following pages.

Bailey had a routine that helped him to deal with the long school day. He would hurry home, drop his bag by the door, and sit in front of the television, playing his video games from 3:30 p.m. until he was called to dinner. Each day, Bailey sat entranced, trying to master his latest game.

This particular day, although graphics were flashing across the television screen and bleeps and explosions could be heard coming from it, Bailey was nowhere to be seen. If anyone had walked past and looked closely at the screen, they would have seen Bailey shielding himself behind a tall, white pillar. Enormous, glowing orange boulders, straight from the pit of a volcano, were rolling toward him. The pillar next to Bailey's was struck by a fiery boulder, shattering it into hundreds of pieces and causing a loud explosion.

"This has to be a dream!" Bailey thought to himself. "It just has to be!"

Bailey looked around at the strange world he found himself in. The sky was coal-black and absent of stars. The ground was a brilliant, emerald green, completely flat and so hard it felt like glass. Although he struggled to believe it, Bailey recognized the scenery as one constructed using the latest computer graphics.

Bailey squeezed his eyes shut and thought, "How can I be inside a game?"

He slowly opened his eyes, wishing that the living room he spent every afternoon sitting in would appear. Instead, a strange-looking monkey wearing red overalls was staring angrily at him.

Woosh!

A very shiny and extremely sharp, star-shaped object spun dangerously close to

Bailey's left ear. The monkey reached into its backpack to retrieve another. Bailey, not waiting around for the monkey's aim to improve, turned and ran. Another star skimmed by his right knee. Bailey jumped up and somehow managed to keep running in midair. He spotted a boulder that had changed from sizzling orange to an earthy brown. It looked safe enough, so he hid behind it.

"This . . . is . . . not . . ." Bailey started to say, but he couldn't catch his breath to speak. He was wheezing heavily, his chest heaving, and sweat ran into his eyes.

"If I ever get out of here," Bailey thought to himself, "I promise to play outside more and play less video games!"

Instantly, Bailey felt a strange pulling sensation in his stomach. It was as if something was trying to turn him inside out.

In a flash, Bailey found himself sitting cross-legged on the carpet in front of the television. As if it were a snake about to bite him, Bailey dropped the game controller from his hands. He leaned forward and turned the television off.

He spotted the cover of the game he had been playing and remembered that a man had handed it to him outside the entrance of his favorite game store. The game was called: "CHANGE YOUR LIFE," and on the cover in red letters were the words . . . *Warning: This game will lead to a happier, healthier life.*

Bailey stood up on his weak, shaky legs and walked toward the glass sliding door that opened out to the back yard. Through it, he could see his sister and his dad kicking the soccer ball to one another. He took a deep breath and opened the door to join them.

CHANGE YOUR LIFE!

Literal   Find the answers directly in the text.

1. Order the events from 1 to 5.

    a. _____ A monkey tries to attack Bailey.

    b. _____ Bailey arrives home from school.

    c. _____ A pillar is struck by a fiery boulder and explodes.

    d. _____ Bailey drops the game controller.

    e. _____ Bailey hides behind a boulder.

2. What made Bailey jump and run in midair?

_____

_____

_____

Inferential   Think about what the text says.

1. Do you think Bailey enjoyed school? Copy the sentence from the text that supports your claim.

_____

_____

2. Why do you think Bailey couldn't catch his breath to speak after running away from the monkey?

_____

_____

3. Explain how Bailey's feelings toward his video games changed during the story.

_____

_____

CHANGE YOUR LIFE!

Applied   Use what you know about the text and your own experience.

1. List words and phrases to describe how you think the man who handed Bailey the "CHANGE YOUR LIFE" game feels about video games.

   _____

   _____

   _____

   _____

   _____

2. Do you think Bailey will keep his promise? Explain your answer.

   _____

   _____

   _____

   _____

   _____

   _____

   _____

3. In what ways do you think Bailey's life will change?

   _____

   _____

   _____

   _____

   _____

CHANGE YOUR LIFE!

Refer to the text on page 105 to help you with this activity. Bailey did keep his promise to play more outside and spend less time playing video games. When he was older, Bailey decided that other children should learn about his story so he decided to write to the Better Health Production Company.

1. Write a paragraph that summarizes Bailey's story and explains how it affected his life.

_____

_____

_____

_____

_____

2. The production company accepts Bailey's proposal to make the film *Change Your Life!,* and designers create a storyboard of four of the main scenes in the film. Draw and write about these four scenes from the film.

Scene 1

_____

Scene 2

_____

Scene 3

_____

Scene 4

_____

Common Core State Standards

Standards Correlations

Each lesson meets one or more of the following Common Core State Standards © Copyright 2010. National Governors Association Center for Best Practices and Council of Chief State School Officers. All rights reserved. For more information about the Common Core State Standards, go to *http://www.corestandards.org/* or *http://www.teachercreated.com/standards.*

Reading Literature/Fiction Text Standards	Text Title	Pages
Key Ideas and Details		
ELA.RL.5.1 Quote accurately from a text when explaining what the text says explicitly and when drawing inferences from the text.	The Babysitter's Revenge The Farmer, His Son, and a Donkey Sarah and the Secret Castle The Great Race The Dolphin Mystery Bowey Island The Troll/Different The Giant with Teeth of Fire Stop Clowning Around! Superstitious The First Spider Change Your Life!	14–18 19–23 24–28 29–33 34–38 39–43 49–53 54–58 59–63 69–73 94–98 104–108
ELA.RL.5.2 Determine a theme of a story, drama, or poem from details in the text, including how characters in a story or drama respond to challenges or how the speaker in a poem reflects upon a topic; summarize the text.	The Babysitter's Revenge The Farmer, His Son, and a Donkey Sarah and the Secret Castle The Great Race The Dolphin Mystery Bowey Island The Troll/Different The Giant with Teeth of Fire Stop Clowning Around! Superstitious The First Spider Change Your Life!	14–18 19–23 24–28 29–33 34–38 39–43 49–53 54–58 59–63 69–73 94–98 104–108
ELA.RL.5.3 Compare and contrast two or more characters, settings, or events in a story or drama, drawing on specific details in the text (e.g., how characters interact).	The Babysitter's Revenge The Farmer, His Son, and a Donkey The Dolphin Mystery The Troll/Different Stop Clowning Around! The First Spider Change Your Life!	14–18 19–23 34–38 49–53 59–63 94–98 104–108

Reading Literature/Fiction Text Standards *(cont.)*	Text Title	Pages
Craft and Structure		
ELA.RL.5.4 Determine the meaning of words and phrases as they are used in a text, including figurative language such as metaphors and similes.	Sarah and the Secret Castle The Dolphin Mystery The Troll/Different The Giant with Teeth of Fire Superstitious The First Spider Change Your Life!	24–28 34–38 49–53 54–58 69–73 94–98 104–108
ELA.RL.5.5 Explain how a series of chapters, scenes, or stanzas fits together to provide the overall structure of a particular story, drama, or poem.	The Farmer, His Son, and a Donkey The Great Race The Troll/Different The Giant with Teeth of Fire Superstitious	19–23 29–33 49–53 54–58 69–73
ELA.RL.5.6 Describe how a narrator's or speaker's point of view influences how events are described.	The Farmer, His Son, and a Donkey Sarah and the Secret Castle The Great Race The Dolphin Mystery The First Spider Change Your Life!	19–23 24–28 29–33 34–38 94–98 104–108
Integration of Knowledge and Ideas		
ELA.RL.5.7 Analyze how visual and multimedia elements contribute to the meaning, tone, or beauty of a text (e.g., graphic novel, multimedia presentation of fiction, folktale, myth, poem).	The Giant with Teeth of Fire Change Your Life!	54–58 104–108
Range of Reading and Level of Text Complexity		
ELA.RL.5.10 By the end of the year, read and comprehend literature, including stories, dramas, and poetry, at the high end of the grades 4–5 text complexity band independently and proficiently.	The Babysitter's Revenge The Farmer, His Son, and a Donkey Sarah and the Secret Castle The Great Race The Dolphin Mystery Bowey Island The Troll/Different The Giant with Teeth of Fire Stop Clowning Around! Superstitious The First Spider Change Your Life!	14–18 19–23 24–28 29–33 34–38 39–43 49–53 54–58 59–63 69–73 94–98 104–108

Common Core State Standards *(cont.)*

Reading Informational Text/Nonfiction Standards	Text Title	Pages
Key Ideas and Details		
ELA.RI.5.1 Quote accurately from a text when explaining what the text says explicitly and when drawing inferences from the text.	A Long Way from Home Bakerstown Council The Saltshaker Trick Cinema Situation Leonardo da Vinci The Painting in the Shed Blaze Destroys School Firstborn Fury!	9–13 44–48 64–68 74–78 79–83 84–88 89–93 99–103
ELA.RI.5.2 Determine two or more main ideas of a text and explain how they are supported by key details; summarize the text.	A Long Way from Home Bakerstown Council The Saltshaker Trick Cinema Situation Leonardo da Vinci The Painting in the Shed Blaze Destroys School Firstborn Fury!	9–13 44–48 64–68 74–78 79–83 84–88 89–93 99–103
ELA.RI.5.3 Explain the relationships or interactions between two or more individuals, events, ideas, or concepts in a historical, scientific, or technical text based on specific information in the text.	A Long Way from Home Bakerstown Council The Saltshaker Trick Cinema Situation Leonardo da Vinci The Painting in the Shed	9–13 44–48 64–68 74–78 79–83 84–88
Craft and Structure		
ELA.RI.5.4 Determine the meaning of general academic and domain–specific words and phrases in a text relevant to a *grade 5 topic or subject area.*	Bakerstown Council Cinema Situation Leonardo da Vinci The Painting in the Shed Blaze Destroys School Firstborn Fury!	44–48 74–78 79–83 84–88 89–93 99–103
ELA.RI.5.5 Compare and contrast the overall structure (e.g., chronology, comparison, cause/effect, problem/ solution) of events, ideas, concepts, or information in two or more texts.	A Long Way from Home Bakerstown Council	9–13 44–48

Reading Informational Text/Nonfiction Standards *(cont.)*	Text Title	Pages
Integration of Knowledge and Ideas		
ELA.RI.5.8 Explain how an author uses reasons and evidence to support particular points in a text, identifying which reasons and evidence support which point(s).	A Long Way from Home Bakerstown Council Cinema Situation Leonardo da Vinci Blaze Destroys School Firstborn Fury!	9–13 44–48 74–78 79–83 89–93 99–103
Range of Reading and Level of Text Complexity		
ELA.RI.5.10 By the end of the year, read and comprehend informational texts, including history/social studies, science, and technical texts, at the high end of the grades 4–5 text complexity band independently and proficiently.	A Long Way from Home Bakerstown Council The Saltshaker Trick Cinema Situation Leonardo da Vinci The Painting in the Shed Blaze Destroys School Firstborn Fury!	9–13 44–48 64–68 74–78 79–83 84–88 89–93 99–103